KOMPAKT-WISSEN ENGLISCH

Rainer Jacob

Grundwortschatz

Die wichtigsten 1000 Wörter

W0371573

STARK

Umschlagbild
Gestaltungselement Flagge: © Carsten Reisinger – Fotolia.com

www.stark-verlag.de
1. Auflage 2010

Inhalt

Autor: Rainer Jacob

Vorwort

Liebe Schülerin, lieber Schüler,

du hast sicher schon gemerkt, wie wichtig ein umfangreicher Wortschatz ist; egal, ob es darum geht, einen Text zu verstehen, Fragen zu beantworten oder selbst Texte zu verfassen. Mit diesem Band kannst du die 1000 wichtigsten Vokabeln und Idioms aus dem Wortschatz der 5. bis 8. Klasse Realschule ganz leicht lernen oder wieder auffrischen. Somit bist du optimal auf den Unterricht und auf Klassenarbeiten vorbereitet.

Der übersichtliche Aufbau erleichtert dir die Arbeit:

- Die **Vokabeln** zu den wichtigsten im Unterricht behandelten Themen findest du **übersichtlich und thematisch geordnet** zusammengestellt. Als Wortfelder aufbereitet kannst du sie so leichter lernen. Zum Einprägen helfen dir auch die deutsche Bedeutung und der angegebene **Beispielsatz**: erst durch die Einbettung des Wortes in einen sinnvollen Zusammenhang siehst du, wie du das Wort verwenden kannst.
- Zum gezielten Nachschlagen und Wiederholen findest du am Ende des Buches eine **alphabetische Liste des kompletten Grundwortschatzes** sowie der wichtigsten **unregelmäßigen Verben**. Somit kannst du eventuelle Lücken ganz schnell schließen.

Um gezielt einzelne Kapitel zu wiederholen, gehe Wort für Wort vor und bilde selbst englische Sätze, die du mit den angegebenen Beispielsätzen vergleichst. Wenn du deinen gesamten Wortschatz auffrischen willst, lies dir die Beispielsätze durch oder decke einzelne Spalten ab. Auch wenn du in der Schule bis jetzt noch nicht alle Wörter gelernt haben solltest, kannst du mit deinem neuen Buch arbeiten: Wiederhole die, die du schon kennst, und versuche, dir auch ein paar neue Vokabeln einzuprägen. Ich bin mir sicher, dass du sie sehr bald brauchen kannst.

Jetzt wünsche ich dir viel Erfolg für deine Klassenarbeiten und vor allem viel Spaß beim Erweitern und Auffrischen deines Wortschatzes!

Rainer Jacob

Abkürzungsverzeichnis

AE	American English
BE	British English
a.m.	vormittags
p.m.	nachmittags
jdm.	jemandem
jdn.	jemanden
Sg.	Singular
Pl.	Plural
s.o.	someone
sth.	something

Family and Friends

vocabulary	dt. Bedeutung	English sentence
alone	*allein*	I don't like being alone at home.
aunt	*Tante*	My mother's or my father's sister is my aunt.
birth	*Geburt*	On December 24, people in Germany celebrate the birth of Jesus.
(to) give birth	*zur Welt bringen*	His mother gave birth to four children.
birthday	*Geburtstag*	My birthday is in December.
boy	*Junge*	Simon is a five-year-old boy.
boyfriend	*Freund*	Malcolm is Wendy's boyfriend.
(to) break up	*zerbrechen, auseinandergehen*	The marriage between Diana and Charles broke up after 15 years.
bride	*Braut*	The bride looked lovely in her white dress.
bridegroom	*Bräutigam*	The bridegroom was very nervous.
brother	*Bruder*	Poppy has two brothers, Simon and Felix.
child children [Pl.]	*Kind* *Kinder*	Children are our future.
couple	*Paar*	Marc and Lena are a nice couple.
cousin	*Cousin/-e*	My cousin Phil is the son of my aunt Jemma.
dad	*Papa*	If I want to know something, I can always ask my dad.
date of birth	*Geburtsdatum*	My sister's date of birth is 3 January, 1998.
daughter	*Tochter*	The Millers have two daughters: Grace and Lena.
(to) divorce	*sich scheiden lassen*	When Sue was twelve her parents divorced.

vocabulary	dt. Bedeutung	English sentence
divorced	*geschieden*	He isn't married any more, he's divorced.
(to) get engaged	*sich verloben*	When people get engaged they want to marry soon.
family	*Familie*	My mother's family was very poor.
family member	*Familienangehörige/-r*	For my grandmother's birthday all the family members come together.
father	*Vater*	My father works in the city.
favour	*Gefallen, Gefälligkeit*	Could you please do me a favour?
first name	*Vorname*	Three girls in my class have the same first name: Amy.
friend	*Freund/-in*	Nobody wants to be without friends.
friendly	*freundlich*	Friendly people smile a lot.
friendship	*Freundschaft*	My friendship with Tom began when we were seven.
gentleman	*Herr, Kavalier, Gentleman*	My grandfather is a real gentleman: he always lets ladies go first.
girl	*Mädchen*	There's a new girl in my class.
girlfriend	*Freundin*	Chris has found a new girlfriend.
grandad	*Opa*	My grandad gave me an extra £ 10.
grandchild	*Enkelkind*	Our neighbour, Mr Myers, has twelve grandchildren.
granddaughter	*Enkelin*	The granddaughter of Mr Jones is only two years old.
grandfather	*Großvater*	I usually call my grandfather "Grandad".
grandmother	*Großmutter*	My grandmother is my grandfather's wife. I call her "Grandma".
grandparents	*Großeltern*	My mum's or my dad's parents are my grandparents.
grandson	*Enkel*	Mr Keenan is very proud of his grandson.

vocabulary	dt. Bedeutung	English sentence
honeymoon	*Flitterwochen*	Many people spend their honeymoon on the Hawaiian islands.
husband	*Ehemann*	Mr and Mrs Miller are husband and wife.
kid	*Kind, Jugendliche/-r*	Some toys are not only for kids.
lady	*Dame*	Yesterday I helped an old lady across the road.
(to) live together	*zusammenleben*	Today many couples live together even if they are not married.
(to) make friends	*Freundschaft schließen*	Brian is a very friendly boy and that's why he makes friends very quickly.
(to) be married	*verheiratet sein*	My sister has been married for two years now.
(to) marry	*heiraten*	Sue doesn't want to marry before she is 25.
member	*Mitglied*	I'm a member of our football club.
mother	*Mutter*	My mother comes from Scotland.
neighbour	*Nachbar/-in*	We help our neighbours and they help us, too.
nephew	*Neffe*	Harry is the son of my sister Jane. He is my nephew.
niece	*Nichte*	Hillary is the daughter of my brother Ed. She is my niece.
old	*alt*	How old are you?
older	*älter*	When I'm older I want to be a doctor.
parents	*Eltern*	My parents are quite strict and don't allow me to go out.
place of birth	*Geburtsort*	New York is Stuart's place of birth.
(to) be related	*verwandt sein*	There are two pupils in my class who have the same last name, but they are not related.

vocabulary	dt. Bedeutung	English sentence
project	*Projekt, Vorhaben*	We're starting a new project about TV and comics next week.
pupil	*Schüler/-in*	There are 1,500 pupils at my school.
question	*Frage*	Try to answer the questions on the text.
quiet	*still, ruhig*	Our teacher often asks us to be quiet.
research (to) do research	*Forschung* *nachforschen, erforschen, untersuchen*	We sometimes do research on the internet.
rubber [BE]	*Radiergummi*	I've just made a mistake. Can I borrow your rubber, please?
ruler	*Lineal*	Use a ruler to draw a straight (*"gerade"*) line.
school	*Schule*	In the UK school starts at 9 o'clock.
school fees	*Schulgeld, Schulgebühren*	At private schools pupils have to pay school fees.
school holiday(s)	*Schulferien*	In my school holidays I visit my aunt in Glasgow.
school meal	*(Mittag)Essen in der Schule*	Sally's favourite school meal is fish and chips.
school report	*Zeugnis*	My sister always gets a good school report.
school trip	*Schulfahrt, Klassenreise*	Many parents say that school trips are expensive.
school uniform	*Schuluniform*	At British schools children wear school uniforms.
sentence	*Satz*	Make five sentences with the verb "to take".
skill	*Fähigkeit, Fertigkeit*	At school we learn skills which will be useful later on.
(to) speak up	*lauter sprechen*	Can you please speak up so that the others can hear you?

vocabulary	dt. Bedeutung	English sentence
speech	*Rede*	Martin L. King's speech "I have a dream" is quite a famous one.
(to) spell	*richtig schreiben, buchstabieren*	How do you spell this word, please?
spelling	*Rechtschreibung*	Jayden makes too many spelling mistakes in his dictations.
staff-room	*Lehrerzimmer*	Our teachers have a coffee machine in the staff-room.
strict	*streng*	Mr Greaves is a very strict teacher.
student	*Student/-in, Schüler/-in*	Ian is a student at Oxford University.
(to) study	*lernen, studieren*	Jenny wants to have good marks; she studies very hard.
subject	*Schulfach*	History is my favourite subject.
(to) take an exam	*eine Prüfung machen*	British school children take their first exam when they are 7.
talent	*Begabung*	Sophia has creative talent. She is really good at painting.
test	*Klassenarbeit, Prüfung*	When is the next test?
(to) test	*prüfen, testen*	Test your English vocabulary!
textbook	*Lehrbuch*	Our new English textbook has a lot of pictures and cartoons.
timetable	*Stundenplan*	We will get a new timetable next week.
uniform	*Uniform*	British schoolchildren wear uniforms.
vocabulary	*Wortschatz, Vokabular*	We must learn the new vocabulary.
worksheet	*Arbeitsblatt*	Try to do all the exercises on the worksheet.

Free Time and Hobbies

vocabulary	dt. Bedeutung	English sentence
active	*aktiv*	Most people want to be active in their free time.
activity	*(Freizeit)Beschäftigung, Tätigkeit*	Sports are an important school activity.
amazing	*erstaunlich*	The London Planetarium is an amazing place.
boring	*langweilig*	Some people find collecting stamps boring.
box office	*Kasse*	The box office opens at 6 o'clock.
canoeing	*Kanufahren*	In the summer Julianne goes canoeing with her brother and father.
(to) collect	*sammeln*	My little sister collects stickers.
computer games	*Computerspiele*	Neil likes playing computer games.
cooking	*Kochen*	Cooking is my father's hobby.
(to) do aerobics	*Aerobic machen*	My neighbour does aerobics three times a week.
(to) do sport	*Sport treiben*	You should do more sport to keep fit.
entertaining	*unterhaltsam*	Many people find quiz shows on TV entertaining.
entertainment	*Unterhaltung*	He's in the entertainment industry; he makes films.
equipment	*Ausrüstung*	I must buy new tennis equipment.
exciting	*spannend, aufregend*	Standing at the rim ("*Rand*") of the Grand Canyon is exciting.
exercise	*(körperliche) Bewegung, Training, Gymnastik*	Jean does a lot of exercise every week.

vocabulary	dt. Bedeutung	English sentence
(to) exercise	*trainieren, üben*	If you want to become better, you must exercise every day.
experience	*Erfahrung*	Our trip to Scotland was a beautiful experience.
favourite	*Lieblings-*	Reading books is Susan's favourite hobby.
(to) be fun	*Spaß machen*	A visit to the zoo is great fun.
game	*Spiel*	I like playing games with my friends.
gardening	*Gartenarbeit*	My mother likes gardening because of the fresh air.
(to) get away	*entfliehen, entkommen*	At weekends we often try to get away from the city.
(to) go for a walk	*einen Spaziergang machen*	My grandfather goes for a walk in the afternoon.
(to) go window shopping	*einen Schaufenster-bummel machen*	Especially around Christmas it's nice to go window shopping.
health	*Gesundheit*	My grandmother worries about her health.
healthy	*gesund*	Keep your body fit and healthy!
helmet	*Helm*	Wear a helmet to protect your head.
indoors	*drinnen, im Haus*	On cold days we stay indoors.
inline-skating	*Inlineskating*	Wear a helmet when you go inline-skating.
(to) be interested in	*Interesse haben an*	My sister is really interested in music and films.
invitation	*Einladung*	I sent an invitation to my classmates.
(to) invite	*einladen*	I want to invite all my friends to my birthday party.
jogging	*Jogging*	When I go jogging I am always out of breath.
(to) join	*beitreten, mitmachen*	I joined our school band.

vocabulary	dt. Bedeutung	English sentence
(to) keep fit	*fit, gesund bleiben*	Mike goes to a fitness centre three times a week to keep fit.
(to) keep s.o. waiting	*jdn. warten lassen*	When I have a meeting I am always on time. I don't want to keep people waiting.
leisure (time)	*Freizeit*	How do you spend your leisure time?
(to) listen to music	*Musik hören*	Ken's hobby is listening to music.
(to) look forward to	*sich freuen auf*	James and Laura are looking forward to their trip to the sea.
(to) meet friends	*Freunde treffen*	I meet my friends in our youth club every Saturday.
member	*Mitglied*	Helena is a member of our youth club.
mobile phone	*Handy, Mobiltelefon*	Most kids already have a mobile phone or smartphone.
mountain biking	*Mountainbiken*	We go mountain biking in Scotland.
outdoors	*draußen, im Freien*	When it's warm we play outdoors.
(to) paint	*malen*	Painting pictures is not as easy as it seems.
pastime	*Zeitvertreib*	Chess is my favourite pastime.
pen friend	*Brieffreund/-in*	My French pen friend is called Michelle DuBois.
(to) phone friends	*Freunde anrufen*	I always phone my friends when something exciting has happened.
(to) play a musical instrument	*ein Musikinstrument spielen*	Playing a musical instrument can be very relaxing.
(to) play in a band	*in einer Band spielen*	My brother Christopher plays in our school band.
(to) play on the computer	*am Computer spielen*	My mother says I play on my computer too often.

vocabulary	dt. Bedeutung	English sentence
(to) play the guitar	*Gitarre spielen*	My friend Layla plays the guitar in a famous band.
(to) play the piano	*Klavier spielen*	My dad plays the piano beautifully.
popular	*beliebt*	Walking is a popular leisure activity.
(to) practise [BE] **(to) practice** [AE]	*üben*	If you want to win, you have to practise hard.
(to) practise (a sport, hobby)	*ausüben*	Most teenagers like to practise a sport or hobby.
(to) relax	*sich entspannen*	Relax, take it easy.
(to) ride a bike	*Fahrrad fahren*	Riding a bike is much better for you than driving a car.
rule	*Regel, Vorschrift*	You must always keep to the rules of a game.
sight	*Sehenswürdigkeit*	When I go to a new city, I want to see the sights.
(to) go sightseeing	*besichtigen*	Millions of tourists go sightseeing in London.
(to) skateboard	*Skateboard fahren*	My favourite activity is skate-boarding.
sleeping bag	*Schlafsack*	When you go camping, remember to take a warm sleeping bag.
stay	*Aufenthalt*	During our stay in London we went to see Buckingham Palace.
(to) stay at a hotel	*in einem Hotel wohnen*	Camping is more fun than staying at a hotel.
(to) surf the internet	*im Internet surfen*	Surfing the internet is no longer expensive.
(to) take a break	*eine Pause machen*	If I'm tired, I take a break.
(to) take off	*starten*	Our plane takes off at 6 in the morning.

vocabulary	dt. Bedeutung	English sentence
(to) take part in	*teilnehmen an*	All my friends will take part in our trip to Cornwall.
(to) take photos	*Fotos machen*	Sue takes photos for the school newspaper.
(to) take place	*stattfinden*	The Olympic Games take place every four years.
time	*Zeit*	I almost forgot what time it was.
(to) have a great time	*Spaß haben*	We had such a great time at the zoo.
tourism	*Tourismus*	Tourism brings money to poor countries.
tourist	*Tourist/-in*	Millions of tourists fly to faraway countries every year.
tourist attraction	*Touristenattraktion*	Disneyland is a tourist attraction.
(to) travel	*reisen*	In the summer we often travel to the Scottish Highlands.
viewer	*Zuschauer/-in*	All TV viewers like good films.
(to) visit	*besuchen*	On our trip to London we visited the Tower.
(to) watch birds	*Vögel beobachten*	My cousin watches birds and knows all their names.
(to) watch TV	*fernsehen*	My grandad's hobby is watching TV.
(to) work out	*trainieren*	My mother works out at the fitness centre.
youth club	*Jugendclub*	Kevin and his friends meet at the local youth club.
youth hostel	*Jugendherberge*	Our class stayed at a youth hostel in Devon.

Sport

vocabulary	dt. Bedeutung	English sentence
activity	*(Freizeit)Beschäftigung, Tätigkeit*	Sports are an important school activity.
athlete	*Athlet/-in*	Good athletes earn a lot of money.
athletics	*Leichtathletik*	British children can practise athletics at school.
(to) attract	*anziehen*	A Champions' League match always attracts lots of spectators.
attraction	*Attraktion, Sehenswürdigkeit*	The Scottish Highland Games are a major tourist attraction.
ball game	*Ballspiel*	Most kids like ball games.
bat	*Schläger*	A bat is a piece of wood that you use to hit the ball in some games, for example baseball.
(to) be fun	*Spaß machen*	Playing football with my friends is great fun.
(to) be on a team	*in einer Mannschaft sein*	My sister would love to be on the volleyball team.
boxing	*Boxen*	Boxing was Muhammad Ali's job.
breath	*Atem*	After running I am usually out of breath.
(to) breathe	*atmen*	My mum likes going for a walk and breathing in the fresh air.
canoeing	*Kanufahren*	In the summer Julianne goes canoeing with her brother and father.
(to) celebrate	*feiern*	Our team celebrated the victory.
champion	*Sieger/-in, Meister*	Lots of athletes dream of becoming Olympic champions.

vocabulary	dt. Bedeutung	English sentence
changing room	*Umkleidekabine*	After a football match our changing room is always a complete mess.
(to) cheer	*anfeuern*	The fans cheer and encourage their team.
(to) climb	*klettern, besteigen*	On May 29, 1953, Sir Edmund Hillary and Tenzing Norgay climbed Mount Everest for the first time.
coach	*Trainer/-in*	Jack Straw is my tennis coach.
(to) compete	*wetteifern, konkurrieren*	In hockey we compete with two other schools in the neighbourhood.
competition	*Wettkampf*	Heather takes part in the swimming competition.
competitor	*Konkurrent/-in, Wettbewerber/-in*	Henry tries to be better than his competitor.
crowd	*Menschenmenge, Zuschauermenge*	There are always big crowds at international football matches.
cup final	*Pokalendspiel*	Manchester United won the cup final.
cycling	*Radfahren*	My friend Jeremy goes cycling in the French Alps.
(to) dive	*tauchen*	Do you know how to dive?
(to) do aerobics	*Aerobic machen*	My neighbour does aerobics three times a week.
(to) do sport	*Sport treiben*	Do more sport to keep fit.
draw	*Unentschieden*	The football match ended in a draw.
entrance	*Eintritt*	Entrance is free for children under 14.
equipment	*Ausrüstung*	Very good athletes get their equipment for free from sponsors.
event	*Ereignis*	The Tour de France is a famous cycling event.
exciting	*aufregend, spannend*	I find football matches exciting.

vocabulary	dt. Bedeutung	English sentence
famous	*berühmt*	Manchester United is a famous English football club.
favourite	*Lieblings-*	Basketball is my favourite sport.
fight	*Kampf, Schlägerei*	Suddenly a fight broke out.
(to) fight	*kämpfen*	In a boxing match, the competitors fight each other with their fists.
final	*Endspiel*	It is very hard to get into the final.
football	*Fußball*	All over the world people play football.
game	*Spiel*	Rugby is a rough game.
(to) have games	*Sport haben*	When do we have games?
ground	*Stadion*	Chelsea FC's home ground is called "Stamford Bridge".
gymnastics	*Turnen*	I sometimes watch gymnastics on TV.
hero **heroes** [Pl.]	*Held* *Helden*	In 1967 Francis Chichester sailed alone around the world. He was a real hero.
heroine	*Heldin*	My mum admired Steffi Graf – she was her childhood heroine.
(to) hit the ball	*den Ball schlagen, treffen*	Tennis players hit the ball hard.
hooligan	*Rowdy*	Young football hooligans often get into trouble with the police.
indoor	*Innen-, Hallen-*	Squash is an indoor sport.
inline-skating	*Inlineskating*	Jill and Daniel go inline-skating.
(to) join	*beitreten, mitmachen*	I joined our local swimming club.
(to) keep fit	*fit, gesund bleiben*	Meryl goes to a fitness centre three times a week to keep fit.
(to) kick (a ball)	*einen Ball spielen*	My dad knows how to kick a ball.
(to) kick s.o. off a team	*jdn. aus dem Team werfen*	John was never on time for training. That's why he was kicked off the team.

vocabulary	dt. Bedeutung	English sentence
(to) talk	*sprechen*	Marc and Lena talk to each other over the internet.
technical	*technisch, technologisch*	My older sister helps me with any technical problems.
technology	*Technik, Technologie*	Young people are interested in new technology.
(to) text	*eine SMS/Kurznachricht senden*	Please text us what you think about our programme.
text message	*SMS, Kurznachricht*	Many people write text messages more often than letters.
(to) turn off	*abschalten*	When I do my homework I turn off the radio.
(to) turn on	*einschalten*	When my mother works in the kitchen she turns on the radio.
TV	*Fernseher, Fernsehen*	Every evening at nine Mrs Shivers turns on her TV to watch the news.
(to) type in	*eintippen*	To start the programme you have to type in your name.
(to) understand	*verstehen*	My grandad does not understand why I like computer games.
(to) warn	*warnen*	My mum always warns me about the dangers of the internet.
(to) waste	*verschwenden*	"Don't waste too much time playing games on the internet," my mum always says.
waste of time	*Zeitverschwendung*	Many people think that surfing the net is a waste of time.
(to) watch TV	*fernsehen*	My grandparents watch TV in the afternoon.
website	*Seite im Internet*	Our school has its own website.

Unregelmäßige Verben

nfinitive	Past Tense	Past Participle	deutsche Übersetzung
be	was/were	been	*sein*
beat	beat	beaten	*schlagen*
become	became	become	*werden*
begin	began	begun	*beginnen, anfangen*
bend	bent	bent	*biegen*
bet	bet	bet	*wetten*
blow	blew	blown	*blasen*
break	broke	broken	*brechen*
bring	brought	brought	*bringen*
build	built	built	*bauen*
burn	burnt/ed	burnt/ed	*brennen, verbrennen*
buy	bought	bought	*kaufen*
catch	caught	caught	*fangen*
choose	chose	chosen	*wählen*
ome	came	come	*kommen*
ost	cost	cost	*kosten*
ut	cut	cut	*schneiden*
do	did	done	*machen, tun*
draw	drew	drawn	*zeichnen, ziehen*
dream	dreamt/ed	dreamt/ed	*träumen*
drink	drank	drunk	*trinken*
drive	drove	driven	*fahren*
at	ate	eaten	*essen*
all	fell	fallen	*fallen*
eed	fed	fed	*füttern*

afraid	*verängstigt*
after	*nach*
afternoon	*Nachmittag*
afterwards	*nachher, hinterher*
again	*wieder, noch einmal*
against	*gegen*
age	*Alter*
agency	*Agentur*
ago	*vor (… Jahren)*
(to) agree	*übereinstimmen*
agreement	*Vereinbarung*
ahead	*vorn, in Führung*
aim	*Ziel*
(to) aim	*zielen*
air	*Luft*
airport	*Flughafen*
album	*Album*
A-levels	*(etwa) Abitur*
alcohol	*Alkohol*
alive	*lebendig, (noch) am Leben*
all	*alle, alles*
all over the world	*auf der ganzen Welt*
(to) allow	*erlauben, ermöglichen*
almost	*fast, beinahe*
alone	*allein*
along	*vorwärts*
already	*schon, bereits*
also	*auch, ebenfalls, außerdem*
although	*obwohl, obgleich*
always	*immer, ständig*
amazing	*erstaunlich*
ambitious	*ehrgeizig*
ambulance	*Krankenwagen*
among	*unter, untereinander*
amount	*Betrag, Menge*
anger	*Zorn*
angry	*zornig, wütend*
animal	*Tier*
ankle	*Knöchel*
(to) announce	*ankündigen, bekannt geben*
annoyed	*verärgert*
another	*ein(e) andere(r, s), weitere(r, s)*
answer	*Antwort*
(to) answer	*(be)antworten*
anxious	*gespannt*
any	*irgendeine(r, s), jede(r, s), jede(r, s) beliebige*
anybody	*jemand*
anyhow	*sowieso*
anyone	*jede(r)*
anything	*alles*
anyway	*jedenfalls, sowieso, immerhin*
anywhere	*überall*

apart	*getrennt, für sich*
apartment	*Wohnung*
(to) apologize	*sich entschuldigen*
(to) appeal	*jdn. reizen, jdm. gefallen*
(to) appear	*erscheinen*
appearance	*Erscheinung, Erscheinen, Aufkommen*
application	*Bewerbung*
(to) apply (for)	*sich bewerben (um)*
apprentice	*Lehrling, Auszubildende/-r*
apprenticeship	*Berufsausbildung, Lehre*
(to) approve	*billigen*
area	*Gebiet, Bereich*
(to) argue	*argumentieren, sich aussprechen für*
(to) argue	*sich streiten*
argument	*Argument, Begründung, Streit*
arm	*Arm*
armchair	*Sessel*
around	*um … herum*
(to) arrange	*vereinbaren*
arrangement	*Vereinbarung, Anordnung, Vorkehrung*
arrival	*Ankunft*
(to) arrive	*ankommen*
art	*(bildende) Kunst*
article	*Artikel*
artificial	*künstlich, Kunst-*
artist	*Künstler/-in*
as far as	*so weit*
ashamed	*beschämt*
(to) ask	*fragen*
(to) ask for	*bitten um*
assistant	*Assistent/-in, Gehilfe / Gehilfin, Verkäufer/-in*
at last	*endlich*
at least	*wenigstens*
at night	*nachts*
at school	*in der Schule*
at the back	*hinten*
at the front	*vorne*
at work	*bei der Arbeit*
athlete	*Athlet/-in*
athletics	*Leichtathletik*
(to) attach	*etwas befestigen, verbinden, beilegen*
attempt	*Versuch*
(to) attempt	*versuchen*
(to) attend	*besuchen, teilnehmen an*
attention	*Aufmerksamkeit, Beachtung*
attitude	*Haltung, Einstellung*
(to) attract	*anziehen*
attraction	*Attraktion, Sehenswürdigkeit, Anziehungspunkt*

attractive	*attraktiv, anziehend*
audience	*Zuschauer, Publikum*
aunt	*Tante*
au pair	*Au-pair*
author	*Autor/-in*
automatic	*automatisch*
autumn	*Herbst*
available	*erhältlich, verfügbar*
average	*Durchschnitt, durchschnittlich*
(to) avoid	*vermeiden*
(to) awake	*aufwachen, erwachen*
aware	*bewusst*
away	*weg*
back	*zurück, Rücken*
backward	*rückwärts gewandt*
bad	*schlecht, schlimm*
badly	*schlecht*
bag	*Tasche*
baggage [AE]	*Gepäck*
balance	*Gleichgewicht*
balanced	*ausgeglichen*
balcony	*Balkon*
bald	*kahl*
ball game	*Ballspiel*
banana	*Banane*
band	*Band, Gruppe*
bang	*Knall*
bank	*Bank, Ufer*
bar	*Stange, Riegel*
barbecue	*Grillparty*
bare	*bloß, nackt*
base	*Sockel, Basis*
basic	*grundlegend, einfach, grundsätzlich*
basically	*im Wesentlichen, im Grunde*
basis	*Grundlage, Basis*
basket	*Korb*
bat	*Schläger*
bath	*Bad, (Bade)Wanne*
bathroom	*Badezimmer*
battery	*Batterie*
battle	*Schlacht*
(to) be	*sein*
(to) be able to	*können*
(to) be going to	*werden*
(to) be in love with	*lieben, verliebt sein in*
beach	*Strand*
bear	*Bär*
(to) bear	*ertragen*
beard	*Bart*
(to) beat	*schlagen, besiegen*
beautiful	*schön*
because	*weil*
because of	*wegen*
(to) become	*werden*
bed	*Bett*

bedroom	*Schlafzimmer*
beef	*Rindfleisch*
beer	*Bier*
before	*vor*
(to) begin	*anfangen, beginnen*
(to) behave	*sich benehmen*
behaviour	*Verhalten, Benehmen*
behind	*hinten, dahinter, zurück*
belief	*Glaube, Überzeugung*
(to) believe in	*glauben an*
bell	*Glocke, Klingel*
(to) belong to	*angehören, Mitglied sein in*
below	*unten, unter*
belt	*Gürtel*
bench	*Bank (zum Sitzen)*
bend	*Kurve*
(to) bend	*biegen*
benefit	*Nutzen, Vorteil*
beside	*neben*
besides	*außer*
best	*(der/die/das) Beste*
bet	*Wette*
(to) bet	*wetten*
better	*besser*
between	*zwischen*
beyond	*jenseits, darüber hinaus*
bicycle	*Fahrrad*
big	*groß*
bike	*Fahrrad*
bill	*Rechnung, Banknote*
bin	*Mülleimer*
biology	*Biologie*
bird	*Vogel*
biro	*Kugelschreiber*
birth	*Geburt*
birthday	*Geburtstag*
bit	*Stückchen, Stück*
bite	*Biss*
(to) bite	*beißen*
black	*schwarz*
blackboard	*Tafel*
blame	*Schuld*
(to) blame	*die Schuld geben, beschuldigen*
blanket	*Decke*
blind	*blind*
block	*Block, Holzklotz*
block of flats	*Wohnhaus, Mietshaus*
blonde	*blond*
blood	*Blut*
blouse	*Bluse*
(to) blow	*blasen*
blue	*blau, traurig, deprimiert*
(to) blush	*rot werden*
board	*Brett, Tafel*

boarding pass	*Bordkarte*
boarding school	*Internat*
boat	*Boot, Schiff*
body	*Körper*
(to) boil	*kochen, abkochen*
bone	*Knochen*
book	*Buch*
(to) book	*reservieren, buchen*
booking	*Reservierung*
bookshelf	*Bücherregal*
bookshop	*Buchhandlung*
boot	*Stiefel*
border	*Grenze*
bored	*gelangweilt*
boring	*langweilig*
born	*geboren*
borough	*Stadtbezirk*
(to) borrow	*ausleihen*
boss	*Chef/-in*
both	*beide*
(to) bother	*jdn. belästigen*
bottle	*Flasche*
bottom	*Grund, unterster Teil, Boden*
bowl	*Schale, Schüssel, Napf*
box	*Kiste*
boxing	*Boxen*
box office	*Kasse*
boy	*Junge*
boyfriend	*Freund*
brain	*Gehirn, Verstand, Intelligenz*
brake	*Bremse*
(to) brake	*bremsen*
branch	*Zweig, Filiale, Zweigstelle*
brave	*tapfer, mutig*
bread	*Brot*
breadth	*Breite, Weite*
break	*Pause*
(to) break	*brechen, sich etwas brechen*
(to) break up	*zerbrechen, auseinandergehen*
breakdown	*Panne*
breakfast	*Frühstück*
breath	*Atem*
(to) breathe	*atmen*
bride	*Braut*
bridegroom	*Bräutigam*
bridge	*Brücke*
brief	*kurz, bündig*
bright	*hell*
(to) bring	*bringen*
broad	*breit, weit*
(to) broadcast	*senden, übertragen (TV)*
brochure	*Broschüre, Prospekt*

broken	*zerbrochen*
brother	*Bruder*
brown	*braun*
(to) browse	*blättern, schmökern, durchstöbern*
brush	*Bürste*
(to) brush	*bürsten, putzen*
budgie	*Wellensittich*
(to) build	*bauen*
building	*Gebäude, Bau*
bully	*Rüpel, gemeine/-r Mitschüler/-in*
bullying	*Tyrannisieren, Ärgern, Einschüchtern von Mitschülern*
bunch	*Büschel, (Blumen) Strauß*
burden	*Last*
(to) burn	*brennen, verbrennen*
(to) burst	*brechen*
(to) bury	*begraben*
bus	*Omnibus, Schulbus*
by bus	*mit dem Bus*
bush	*Busch, Gebüsch*
business	*Geschäft, Firma*
businessman	*Unternehmer, Geschäftsmann*
business woman	*Geschäftsfrau, Unternehmerin*
bus stop	*Bushaltestelle*
busy	*belebt, beschäftigt*
but	*a.*
butter	*Butt*
button	*Knopf,*
(to) buy	*kaufen*
by birth	*von Geburt*
by mistake	*aus Versehen*
by trade	*von Beruf*
bye-bye	*Auf Wiedersehen*
cable	*Kabel*
café	*Café, kleines Restaurant*
cafeteria	*Kantine, Selbstbedienungsrestaurant*
cage	*Käfig*
cake	*Kuchen*
calculator	*Taschenrechner*
calendar	*Kalender*
call	*Anruf*
(to) call	*anrufen, rufen, nennen*
calm	*ruhig, gelassen*
camera	*Kamera*
camp	*(Trainings, Zelt)Lager*
campsite	*Campingplatz*
can	*können*
can [AE]	*Büchse, Dose*
(to) cancel	*streichen, annullieren, absagen*
candle	*Kerze*
canoeing	*Kanufahren*

	Kantine
…n	Schlucht
	Mütze
…pital	Hauptstadt
captain	Kapitän
caption	Bildunterschrift
car	Auto, Wagen
card	Karte
cardboard	Pappe
care	Betreuung, Aufmerksamkeit
(to) care about	sich kümmern um
career	(berufliche) Laufbahn, Karriere
careers adviser	Berufsberater/-in
careful	vorsichtig
careless	unvorsichtig
carpenter	Tischler/-in
carpet	Teppich
carriage	Wagen, Waggon
(to) carry	tragen
(to) carry out	ausführen
carton	Karton, (Milch-, Saft-)Packung
case	Fall
cash	Bargeld
(to) cash	einlösen
castle	Schloss
cat	Katze
(to) catch	fangen
(to) catch (a bus, a train)	(einen Bus/Zug) erreichen
(to) catch a cold	sich erkälten
cathedral	Kathedrale, Dom
cause	Grund, Anlass
(to) celebrate	feiern
celebration	Feier
centimetre	Zentimeter
central	Zentral-, Mittel-
centre	Mitte, Zentrum
century	Jahrhundert
cereal	Frühstückszerealien (Cornflakes, Müsli)
certain	sicher, gewiss
certainly	sicherlich, gewiss
chair	Stuhl
chalk	Kreide
champion	Meister, Sieger/-in
challenge	Herausforderung
chance	Chance, Möglichkeit
change	Wechsel, Veränderung
(to) change	wechseln, tauschen
(to) change a tyre	einen Reifen wechseln
(to) change trains	umsteigen
changing room	Umkleidekabine
channel	Kanal, Fernsehprogramm
Channel Tunnel	der Ärmelkanaltunnel

dishwasher	*Geschirrspüler*
dislike	*Abneigung*
(to) dislike	*nicht mögen*
display	*(Schaufenster)Auslage*
distance	*Entfernung*
distant	*fern*
(to) disturb	*stören*
(to) dive	*tauchen*
(to) divide	*teilen*
diving	*Tauchen*
division	*Verteilung*
(to) divorce	*sich scheiden lassen*
divorced	*geschieden*
(to) do	*machen, tun*
(to) do a course	*einen Kurs besuchen*
(to) do aerobics	*Aerobic machen*
(to) do (one's) homework	*Hausaufgaben machen*
(to) do research	*nachforschen, erforschen, untersuchen*
(to) do sport	*Sport treiben*
(to) do the shopping	*Einkäufe machen, einkaufen gehen*
(to) do well	*gut abschneiden*
doctor	*Arzt, Ärztin*
dog	*Hund*
(to) be on the dole	*Arbeitslosengeld beziehen*
domestic	*häuslich, Haus-*
door	*Tür*
(to) double	*verdoppeln*
double bed	*Doppelbett*
double-decker	*Doppeldecker*
doubt	*Zweifel*
(to) doubt	*zweifeln*
(to) download	*herunterladen*
downstairs	*unten (im Haus), treppab, die Treppe hinunter*
downtown	*Innenstadt*
drama group	*Theatergruppe*
draw	*Unentschieden*
(to) draw	*zeichnen, ziehen*
drawing	*Zeichnung*
dream	*Traum*
(to) dream	*träumen*
dress	*Kleid*
(to) dress	*sich kleiden*
drink	*Getränk*
(to) drink	*trinken*
drive	*Auffahrt*
(to) drive	*fahren*
(to) drive a car	*Auto fahren*
driver's license [AE], driving licence [BE]	*Führerschein*
driving test	*Führerscheinprüfung*
drop	*Fall, Sturz, Tropfen*
(to) drop	*fallen (lassen)*

(to) drop out of school	*die Schule abbrechen, die Schule vorzeitig verlassen*
(to) drown	*ertrinken, ertränken*
drug	*Droge, Rauschgift*
dry	*trocken*
(to) dry	*trocknen*
dull	*langweilig, eintönig*
during	*während*
dust	*Staub*
dustbin [BE]	*Mülleimer*
duty	*Dienst, Pflicht*
DVD burner	*DVD-Brenner*
DVD drive	*DVD-Laufwerk*
each	*jeder, jede, jedes (einzelne)*
ear	*Ohr*
early	*früh*
(to) earn	*(Geld) verdienen*
(to) earn a living	*seinen Lebensunterhalt verdienen*
earth	*Erde*
east	*östlich, Osten*
easy	*leicht, einfach*
(to) eat	*essen*
edge	*Kante, Rand*
(to) edit	*bearbeiten, redigieren*
education	*Ausbildung, Bildung, Erziehung*
effect	*Wirkung*

effort	*Anstrengung*
e.g.	*z. B. (zum Beispiel)*
egg	*Ei*
either … or …	*entweder … oder …*
elbow	*Ellbogen*
election	*Wahl*
electric(al)	*elektrisch*
electrician	*Elektriker/-in*
electricity	*Elektrizität*
elephant	*Elefant*
elevator [AE]	*Aufzug*
else	*alle anderen, sonst*
e-mail (electronic mail)	*E-Mail*
(to) embarrass	*in Verlegenheit / in eine peinliche Lage bringen*
embarrassed	*verlegen, peinlich berührt*
embarrassing	*peinlich*
emergency	*Notfall*
emigrant	*Auswanderer, Auswanderin*
(to) emigrate	*auswandern*
emigration	*Auswanderung*
emotion	*Gefühl*
emphasis	*Betonung*
(to) emphasize	*betonen*
(to) employ	*beschäftigen, anstellen, verwenden*

(to) be employed	*angestellt sein*
empty	*leer*
(to) encourage	*ermutigen*
encyclopaedia	*Lexikon*
end	*Ende*
enemy	*Feind*
energy	*Energie*
engaged	*verlobt*
engine	*Maschine, Motor*
engineer	*Ingenieur/-in, Techniker/-in*
engineering	*Technik, Maschinenbau*
(to) enjoy	*genießen*
enjoyable	*angenehm, nett, unterhaltsam*
enough	*genügend, ausreichend; genug*
(to) enter	*betreten, einreisen in, teilnehmen an; eintreten*
entertaining	*unterhaltsam*
entertainment	*Unterhaltung*
enthusiastic	*begeistert*
entrance	*Eintritt, Eingang*
entry	*Eintritt*
environment	*Umwelt*
equal	*gleich*
equality	*Gleichheit*
equipment	*Ausrüstung, Ausstattung*
eraser [AE]	*Radiergummi*
error	*Fehler*
escape	*Flucht, Ausbruch*
(to) escape	*entfliehen*
especially	*besonders, insbesondere*
(to) estimate	*(ab)schätzen*
ethnic	*Volks-, ethnisch*
euro	*Euro*
Europe	*Europa*
European	*europäisch, Europäer/-in*
even	*sogar, selbst*
even (number)	*gerade (Zahl)*
evening	*Abend*
in the evening	*abends*
event	*Ereignis*
ever	*je, jemals, schon*
every	*jede(r, s)*
everybody	*jede(r)*
everything	*alles*
everywhere	*überall*
exactly	*genau*
(to) exaggerate	*übertreiben*
exam(ination)	*Prüfung*
(to) examine	*untersuchen*
example	*Beispiel*
excellent	*ausgezeichnet*

except for	*außer, mit Ausnahme von*
exception	*Ausnahme*
excerpt	*Auszug, Ausschnitt*
exchange	*Austausch*
(to) exchange	*tauschen*
exchange programme	*Austauschprogramm*
(to) excite	*auf-, erregen*
excited	*aufgeregt*
exciting	*spannend, aufregend*
excursion	*Ausflug, Exkursion*
(to) excuse	*entschuldigen*
exercise	*(körperliche) Bewegung, Training, Gymnastik*
(to) exercise	*trainieren, üben*
exercise book	*Heft*
exhibition	*Ausstellung*
(to) exist	*existieren, bestehen*
existence	*Dasein, Leben*
exit	*Ausgang*
(to) exit	*verlassen, beenden*
(to) expect	*erwarten*
expectation	*Erwartung*
expensive	*teuer*
experience	*Erfahrung*
experienced	*erfahren*
experiment	*Versuch*
expert	*Fachmann, Fachfrau, Experte, Expertin*
(to) explain	*erklären*
explanation	*Erklärung*
(to) explode	*explodieren*
exploration	*Erforschung*
(to) explore	*erforschen*
explosion	*Explosion*
(to) express	*ausdrücken*
expression	*Ausdruck*
extra	*zusätzlich*
extra classes	*Nachhilfe*
extraordinary	*außerordentlich, außergewöhnlich*
extremely	*äußerst, außerordentlich*
eye	*Auge*
face	*Gesicht*
(to) face	*sich gegenüberstehen, konfrontiert sein mit*
fact	*Tatsache*
factory	*Fabrik*
(to) fail	*(eine Prüfung) nicht bestehen, durchfallen*
failure	*Misserfolg*
fair	*blond, hell, gerecht*
fairly	*ziemlich*
faithful	*treu*
Yours faithfully	*Mit freundlichen Grüßen*
fall	*Absturz*

(to) fall	*fallen*
(to) fall asleep	*einschlafen*
false	*falsch*
fame	*Ruhm*
familiar	*vertraut*
family	*Familie*
family member	*Familien-angehörige/-r*
famous	*berühmt*
fantastic	*toll, fantastisch*
far	*von weit her, weit entfernt*
farm	*Bauernhof, Farm*
farther	*weiter (entfernt)*
farthest	*am weitesten (entfernt)*
fashion	*Mode*
fast	*schnell*
(to) fasten	*festmachen*
fat	*fett, dick*
father	*Vater*
fault	*Fehler*
favour	*Gefallen, Gefälligkeit*
favourable	*günstig*
favourite	*Lieblings-*
fax machine	*Faxgerät*
fear	*Angst*
feature	*Merkmal, Eigen-schaft, Reportage*
February	*Februar*
(to) be fed up with sth.	*etwas satthaben*
fee	*Gebühr*
(to) feed	*ernähren, füttern*
(to) feel	*fühlen*
(to) feel sick	*sich schlecht fühlen, übel sein*
feeling	*Gefühl*
feet	*Füße*
felt-tip pen	*Filzstift*
female	*weiblich*
fence	*Zaun*
ferry	*Fähre*
(to) fetch	*holen*
fever	*Fieber*
few	*wenig/-e*
field	*Wiese, Feld*
fierce	*heftig, scharf, grimmig*
fight	*Kampf, Schlägerei*
(to) fight	*kämpfen, sich prügeln*
figure	*Figur*
file	*Datei*
(to) fill	*füllen*
final	*Endspiel*
finally	*schließlich*
(to) find	*finden*
fine	*Geldstrafe*
fine	*gut, fein, schön*
finger	*Finger*

(to) finish	zu Ende sein, beenden
(to) finish school	die Schule beenden
fire	Feuer
(to) fire	entlassen, feuern
firefighter	Feuerwehrmann/ -frau
firm	Firma
first	erste/-r/-s
first floor	[BE] erster Stock, [AE] Erdgeschoss
first name	Vorname
fish	Fisch
fish fingers	Fischstäbchen
(to) fit	sich eignen, passen
fix	fest
(to) fix	befestigen, reparieren, in Ordnung bringen
flag	Fahne, Flagge
flame	Flamme
flash	(Foto)Blitz
(to) flash	aufleuchten, blinken
flat	flach
flat	Wohnung
(to) flatter	schmeicheln
flavour	Geschmack
(to) flee	fliehen
flight	Flug
(to) float	(an der Oberfläche) schwimmen
flood	Flut, Hochwasser
(to) flood	überfluten
floor	Fußboden, Stockwerk
flour	Mehl
(to) flow	fließen
flower	Blume
(to) fly	fliegen
(to) fold	falten
(to) follow	folgen
fond	liebevoll
food	Essen, Nahrung
fool	Narr, Dummkopf
foot, feet [BE]	Fuß
football	Fußball
(to) force	zwingen
foreign	ausländisch
foreign language	Fremdsprache
forest	Wald
forever	für immer
(to) forget	vergessen
(to) forgive	jdm. verzeihen
for good	endgültig
fork	Gabel
form	Form, Formular
(to) form	bilden
formal	förmlich, formell
former	früher, ehemalig
form teacher	Klassenlehrer/-in
fortunate	glücklich

fortune	*Vermögen*
forward	*nach vorn*
(to) found	*gründen*
fountain pen	*Füller*
frame	*Rahmen*
freak	*Fanatiker/-in*
free	*frei*
free of charge	*kostenlos, gratis*
freedom	*Freiheit*
(to) freeze	*(er)frieren, gefrieren, erstarren*
freight	*Güter, Fracht*
French fries [AE]	*Pommes frites*
frequent	*häufig*
frequently	*oft, häufig*
fresh	*frisch*
fridge	*Kühlschrank*
friend	*Freund/-in*
friendly	*freundlich*
friendship	*Freundschaft*
(to) frighten	*jdn. erschrecken, jdm. Angst machen*
frightened	*verängstigt*
from	*aus, von*
front	*Vorderseite*
front door	*Haustür*
frontier	*Grenzland, Grenze*
(to) frown	*die Stirn runzeln*
fruit	*Obst*
frustrated	*enttäuscht, frustriert*
full	*voll*
full-time	*Vollzeit*
fun	*Spaß*
(to) be fun	*Spaß machen*
funny	*lustig, witzig*
furniture	*Möbel*
further	*weiter (entfernt), ferner*
furthest	*am weitesten (entfernt)*
future	*Zukunft*
gadget	*Gerät, technische Spielerei*
game	*Spiel*
gang	*Bande, Truppe*
gap	*Lücke*
garage	*Garage*
garbage [AE]	*Müll*
garden	*Garten*
gardening	*Gartenarbeit*
gas [AE]	*Benzin*
gate	*Tor, Sperre, Flugsteig*
(to) gather	*sammeln*
general	*allgemein*
generally	*im Allgemeinen*
generation	*Generation, Menschenalter*
generous	*großzügig*
gentle	*sanft, leicht*

gentleman	Herr, Kavalier, Gentleman
genuine	echt
geography	Erdkunde, Geografie
(to) get	bekommen
(to) get away	entfliehen, entkommen
(to) get dressed	sich anziehen
(to) get engaged	sich verloben
(to) get on	auskommen, sich verstehen
(to) get off	aussteigen
(to) get ready	sich fertig machen
(to) get rid of	loswerden
(to) get up	aufstehen
(to) get used to	sich gewöhnen an
ghost	Geist, Gespenst
giant	Riese
gift	Gabe, Begabung
gigantic	riesig, gigantisch
girl	Mädchen
girlfriend	Freundin
(to) give	geben
(to) give a hand	behilflich sein
(to) give birth	zur Welt bringen
(to) give up	aufgeben
glad	froh, erfreut, freudig
glass	Glas
glasses	Brille
global	global, weltweit
globe	Globus, Erdball
glue	Klebstoff
(to) go	gehen
(to) go by bus	mit dem Bus fahren
(to) go for a ride	eine Spazierfahrt machen
(to) go for a walk	einen Spaziergang machen
(to) go off the rails	entgleisen
(to) go on a trip	eine Reise machen, einen Ausflug machen
(to) go on holiday	in Urlaub fahren
(to) go out for a meal	essen gehen
(to) go sightseeing	besichtigen, Sehenswürdigkeiten anschauen
(to) go to bed	zu Bett gehen
(to) go up in price	im Preis steigen, teurer werden
(to) go window shopping	einen Schaufensterbummel machen
goal	Ziel, Tor
gold	Gold
goldfish	Goldfisch
(to) be good at	gut sein in
good-bye	Auf Wiedersehen, Lebe wohl!
goods	Waren, Güter
(to) govern	regieren

government	*Regierung*
grade [AE]	*(Schul)Klasse, Jahrgangsstufe*
gradually	*allmählich*
grammar school	*Gymnasium*
grand	*prächtig, großartig*
grandad	*Opa*
grandchild	*Enkelkind*
granddaughter	*Enkeltochter*
grandfather	*Großvater*
grandma	*Oma*
grandmother	*Großmutter*
grandpa	*Opa*
grandparents	*Großeltern*
grandson	*Enkel*
(to) grant	*gewähren, bewilligen*
grape	*(Wein)Traube*
grass	*Gras*
gravy	*(Braten)Soße*
grateful	*dankbar*
great	*groß, großartig*
green	*grün*
(to) greet	*grüßen*
greeting	*Begrüßung, Gruß*
grey [AE], gray [BE]	*grau*
(to) groan	*stöhnen, ächzen*
ground	*(Erd)Boden, Stadion*
ground floor [BE]	*Erdgeschoss*
group	*Gruppe*
(to) grow	*wachsen*
grown-up	*Erwachsene/-r*
growth	*Wachstum*
guard	*Wache*
(to) guard	*bewachen*
guess	*Vermutung*
(to) guess	*(er)raten, vermuten*
guest	*Gast*
guitar	*Gitarre*
guide	*Reiseführer/-in, Reiseleiter/-in*
(to) guide	*führen, leiten*
guilty	*schuldig*
gun	*(Schuss)Waffe*
guy	*Typ, Bursche*
gymnastics	*Turnen*
habit	*Gewohnheit, Angewohnheit*
(to) hack	*hacken, zerstückeln, in Computer eindringen*
hair	*Haar(e)*
hairdresser	*Friseur/-in*
half	*halb, Hälfte*
half past (eight)	*halb (neun)*
hall	*Flur, Diele*
ham	*Schinken*
hand	*Hand*

(to) handle	*handhaben, behandeln*
(to) hang	*(auf)hängen*
(to) happen	*sich ereignen*
happy	*glücklich, froh*
harbour	*Hafen*
hard	*hart, schwer*
hard disk	*Festplatte*
hardly	*kaum*
hardware	*Eisenwaren, Computerhardware*
harm	*Schaden*
(to) harm	*schaden*
harmful	*schädlich*
harvest	*Ernte*
hat	*Hut*
hate	*Hass*
(to) hate	*hassen*
(to) have	*haben*
(to) have a bath	*ein Bad nehmen*
(to) have a break	*sich ausruhen*
(to) have a cough	*Husten haben*
(to) have a drink	*etwas trinken*
(to) have a good time	*sich amüsieren*
(to) have a great time	*Spaß haben*
(to) have a party	*feiern*
(to) have a rest	*sich ausruhen*
(to) have a shower	*sich duschen*
(to) have games	*Sport haben*
(to) have got	*haben*
(to) have sth. in common	*etwas gemeinsam haben*
(to) have to	*müssen*
head	*Kopf*
headache	*Kopfschmerzen*
headline	*Schlagzeile, Überschrift*
headteacher	*Schulleiter/-in*
headword	*Stichwort (in einem Lexikon), Eintrag*
health	*Gesundheit*
healthy	*gesund*
(to) hear	*hören*
heart	*Herz*
heat	*Hitze*
heavy	*schwer*
height	*Körpergröße*
Hello!	*Hallo, Guten Tag!*
helmet	*Helm*
help	*Hilfe*
(to) help	*helfen*
Help yourself!	*Bediene dich! Greif zu!*
her	*sie, ihr*
here	*hier*
hero, heroes [Pl.]	*Held*

heroine	*Heldin*
hers	*ihre/-r/-s*
herself	*sich*
(to) hesitate	*zögern, zaudern*
(to) hide	*verbergen, sich verstecken*
high	*hoch*
hill	*Hügel*
him	*ihn*
(to) hire	*mieten*
his	*sein(e, s)*
history	*Geschichte*
(to) hit	*schlagen, treffen*
(to) hit the ball	*den Ball schlagen, treffen*
(to) hold	*halten*
hole	*Loch*
holiday(s)	*Ferien, Urlaub*
holiday job	*Ferienjob*
hollow	*hohl*
holy	*heilig*
home	*Zuhause, Heim*
(to) be home	*zu Hause sein*
homeless	*heimatlos, obdachlos*
(to) be homesick	*Heimweh haben*
homework	*Hausaufgaben*
homework diary	*Hausaufgabenheft*
honest	*ehrlich*
honey	*Honig*
honeymoon	*Flitterwochen*
honour	*Ehre*
hope	*Hoffnung*
(to) hope	*hoffen*
horrible	*grauenhaft, scheußlich*
horse	*Pferd*
hospital	*Krankenhaus*
hostage	*Geisel*
hostel	*Heim, Herberge*
hot	*heiß*
hotel	*Hotel*
hour	*Stunde*
house	*Haus*
household	*Haushalt*
househusband	*Hausmann*
housewife	*Hausfrau*
housework	*Hausarbeit*
however	*jedoch*
hug	*Umarmung*
(to) hug	*umarmen*
huge	*riesig*
human	*menschlich*
human being	*Mensch*
hunger	*Hunger*
hungry	*hungrig*
(to) hunt	*jagen*
hurry	*Eile*
(to) hurry	*sich beeilen*

(to) hurt	*(sich) verletzen*
husband	*Ehemann*
ice	*Eis*
ice-cream	*Speiseeis*
idea	*Vorstellung*
ideal	*vorbildlich*
identity	*Identität*
if	*wenn, falls*
(to) ignore	*nicht beachten*
ill	*krank*
illegal	*ungesetzlich, rechtswidrig*
illness	*Krankheit*
image	*Ebenbild, Bild*
imagination	*Fantasie*
(to) imagine	*sich vorstellen*
immediate	*unmittelbar, sofort*
immense	*ungeheuer, unermesslich*
immigrant	*Einwanderer, Einwanderin*
(to) immigrate	*einwandern*
immigration	*Einwanderung*
impatient	*ungeduldig*
importance	*Wichtigkeit*
important	*wichtig*
impossible	*unmöglich*
(to) impress	*imponieren, beeindrucken*
impression	*Eindruck*
impressive	*beeindruckend*
(to) improve	*(sich) verbessern, besser machen/werden*
improvement	*Verbesserung*
(to) include	*einschließen, enthalten, umfassen*
income	*Einkommen*
increase	*Erhöhung, Zunahme*
(to) increase	*zunehmen, steigen*
increasing	*zunehmend, steigend*
indeed	*in der Tat, gewiss*
independence	*Unabhängigkeit*
Independence Day	*(US) Unabhängigkeitstag (4. Juli)*
independent	*unabhängig*
Indian	*indisch, Inder/-in, indianisch, Indianer/-in*
indoor	*Innen-, Hallen-*
indoors	*drinnen, im Haus*
industrial	*industriell*
industry	*Industrie*
in favour of	*für*
influence	*Einfluss*
(to) inform	*informieren, benachrichtigen*
informal	*locker*
information	*Information*
in general	*im Allgemeinen*
inhabitant	*Einwohner/-in*

injection	*Injektion, Spritze*
(to) injure	*verletzen*
njury	*Verletzung*
nline-skating	*Inlineskating*
(to) inquire	*sich erkundigen*
nside	*drinnen*
(to) insist	*bestehen*
nstead of	*stattdessen, anstatt*
nstruction	*Anweisung, Gebrauchsanweisung*
nstrument	*Instrument*
nsurance	*Versicherung*
ntelligent	*klug, intelligent*
to) intend	*beabsichtigen*
nterest	*Interesse, Zins*
to) be interested in	*interessiert sein an, Interesse haben an*
nternet	*Internet*
n the internet	*im Internet*
to) interrupt	*unterbrechen*
nterview	*Interview, Vorstellungsgespräch*
o) introduce	*(jdn., sich) vorstellen*
nvention	*Erfindung*
nvitation	*Einladung*
o) invite	*einladen*
o) involve	*verwickeln*
regular	*unregelmäßig*
land	*Insel*
sue	*Streitfrage*

IT (information technology)	*IT, Informatik*
item	*Ding, Stück*
its	*sein, seine*
jacket	*Jacke, Sakko*
jam	*Marmelade*
January	*Januar*
jar	*Glas, Topf*
jealous (of)	*eifersüchtig (auf)*
Jew	*Jude, Jüdin*
jewellery	*Schmuck*
job	*Arbeit, Tätigkeit, Aufgabe*
jogging	*Jogging*
(to) join	*sich anschließen, beitreten, mitmachen*
joke	*Witz*
journalist	*Journalist/-in*
journey	*Reise*
judge	*Richter/-in*
juice	*Saft*
July	*Juli*
jump	*Sprung*
(to) jump	*springen*
June	*Juni*
junk food	*Nahrung ohne Nährwert*
just	*nur, bloß, einfach*
justice	*Gerechtigkeit*
(to) justify	*rechtfertigen*

keen on	*scharf auf*
(to) keep	*(be)halten*
(to) keep fit	*fit/gesund bleiben*
(to) keep s.o. waiting	*jdn. warten lassen*
key	*Schlüssel*
keyboard	*Tastatur*
keyword	*Schlüsselwort*
kick	*Tritt*
(to) kick	*treten*
(to) kick a ball	*einen Ball spielen*
(to) kick s.o. off a team	*jdn. aus dem Team werfen*
kid	*Kind, Jugendliche/-r*
(to) kill	*töten*
kind	*Art*
kind	*nett, freundlich, liebenswürdig*
kindness	*Freundlichkeit, Liebenswürdigkeit*
king	*König*
kingdom	*Königreich*
kiss	*Kuss*
kitchen	*Küche*
kite	*Drachen*
knee	*Knie*
knife, knives [Pl.]	*Messer*
(to) knock	*klopfen*
(to) know	*wissen*
knowledge	*Kenntnis(se), Wissen*
known	*bekannt*
label	*Etikett*
labour	*Arbeit*
(to) labour	*arbeiten, schuften*
labourer	*Arbeiter/-in, Arbeitskraft*
ladder	*Leiter*
lady	*Dame*
lake	*(Binnen)See*
lamp	*Lampe*
land	*Land*
(to) land	*landen*
language	*Sprache*
language course	*Sprachkurs*
large	*groß*
(to) last	*dauern*
late	*spät*
(to) be late	*zu spät kommen*
lately	*kürzlich, in letzter Zeit*
latest	*das Neueste, neueste(r, s)*
(to) laugh	*lachen*
laughter	*Gelächter*
laundry	*Wäscherei*
law	*Gesetz*
(to) lay	*legen*
(to) lay the table	*den Tisch decken*
lazy	*faul, träge*

(to) lead	*führen, leiten*
leaf, leaves [Pl.]	*Blatt*
leaflet	*Prospekt, Flugblatt*
(to) lean	*lehnen*
(to) learn	*lernen*
east	*am wenigsten*
(to) leave	*(ver)lassen*
(to) leave for school	*zur Schule gehen*
(to) leave school	*die Schule verlassen*
eft	*links*
to) be left	*übrig sein*
eg	*Bein*
egal	*gesetzlich zulässig, legal*
egend	*Legende*
eisure (time)	*Freizeit*
emon	*Zitrone*
emonade	*Limonade*
to) lend	*(ver)leihen*
ength	*Länge*
ess	*weniger*
esson	*Unterrichtsstunde, Lektion*
o) let	*lassen, erlauben, vermieten*
ethal	*tödlich*
etter	*Brief*
etter box	*Briefkasten*

letter of application	*Bewerbungsschreiben*
letter to the editor	*Leserbrief*
lettuce	*(Kopf)Salat*
level	*Höhe, Niveau*
liberty	*Freiheit*
library	*Bücherei*
(to) lie	*lügen, liegen*
life, lives [Pl.]	*Leben*
lift [BE]	*Aufzug, Lift*
(to) lift	*heben*
light	*leicht*
light	*Licht*
(to) light	*anzünden*
like	*als ob, wie*
(to) like	*mögen*
likely	*wahrscheinlich*
limit	*Begrenzung, Limit*
(to) limit	*begrenzen*
line	*Zeile, Reihe, Leitung*
link	*Verbindung*
(to) link	*verbinden*
lion	*Löwe*
lip	*Lippe*
liquid	*Flüssigkeit*
list	*Liste*
(to) list	*auflisten*
(to) listen	*zuhören*

(to) listen to music	*Musik hören*
(to) listen to the radio	*Radio hören*
litre	*Liter*
little	*klein*
(to) live	*leben*
live	*direkt (TV- oder Radiosendung)*
(to) live together	*zusammenleben*
living room	*Wohnzimmer*
(to) load	*laden, ein-, auf-, beladen*
(to) load the dishwasher	*die Spülmaschine einräumen*
local	*örtlich*
lock	*(Tür-)Schloss*
(to) lock	*zuschließen*
locker	*Schließfach*
(to) log in	*einloggen, sich bei einem Computer anmelden*
(to) log on	*sich anmelden, sich einwählen*
lonely	*einsam, allein*
long	*lang*
(to) long (for)	*sich sehnen (nach)*
(to) look	*schauen, sehen*
(to) look after	*sich kümmern um*
(to) look for	*suchen*
(to) look forward to	*sich freuen auf*
(to) look up	*nachschlagen*
loose	*locker, lose*
lorry	*Lastwagen*
(to) lose	*verlieren*
loss	*Verlust*
lot	*viel*
lots of	*jede Menge*
loud	*laut*
love	*Liebe*
(to) love	*lieben*
lovely	*schön, herrlich, hübsch*
low	*niedrig, leise (Stimme)*
luck	*Glück*
Good luck!	*Viel Glück!*
(to) be lucky	*Glück haben*
lunch	*Mittagessen*
lunch time	*Mittagspause*
lungs	*Lunge*
machine	*Maschine*
mad	*verrückt*
magazine	*Zeitschrift*
magic	*Zauber, Magie*
mail	*Post*
mailbox	*Briefkasten*
main	*Haupt-*
mainly	*hauptsächlich*

major	*größer, wichtiger*
majority	*Mehrheit*
(to) make	*machen*
(to) make a speech	*eine Rede halten*
(to) make friends	*Freundschaft schließen*
(to) make the beds	*die Betten machen*
male	*männlich*
man	*Mann, Mensch*
(to) manage	*(etwas) fertigbringen, leiten*
manager	*Leiter/-in, Direktor/-in, Trainer/-in, Geschäftsführer/-in*
manual	*Handbuch, Hand-*
many	*viel*
map	*Landkarte, Stadtplan*
March	*März*
(to) march	*marschieren*
mark [BE]	*Schulnote*
market	*Markt*
marmalade	*(Orangen)Marmelade*
marriage	*Heirat, Ehe*
(to) be married	*verheiratet sein*
(to) marry	*heiraten*
mask	*Maske*
mass	*(kirchliche) Messe*
(to) match	*(farblich) passen*
match	*Spiel, Wettkampf*
mate	*Kamerad/-in, Kumpel*
material	*Material*
maths	*Mathe*
matter	*Angelegenheit*
(to) matter	*von Bedeutung sein*
May	*Mai*
may	*dürfen*
maybe	*vielleicht*
maze	*Irrgarten*
me	*mir, mich*
meal	*Mahlzeit, Essen, Gericht*
(to) mean	*bedeuten, meinen*
meaning	*Sinn, Bedeutung*
means	*Mittel*
means of communication	*Kommunikationsmittel*
means of transport	*Verkehrsmittel*
meanwhile	*inzwischen, unterdessen*
measure	*Maßnahme*
(to) measure	*messen*
meat	*Fleisch*
mechanic	*Mechaniker/-in*
media	*die Medien*
medicine	*Medizin*
(to) meet	*(sich) treffen*
(to) meet friends	*Freunde treffen*

meeting	*Treffen, Versammlung, Zusammenkunft*
(to) melt	*schmelzen*
member	*Mitglied*
memory	*Gedächtnis*
(to) mend	*reparieren, ausbessern*
(to) mention	*erwähnen*
menu	*Speisekarte*
mess	*Unordnung*
(to) mess	*durcheinanderbringen, Unordnung machen*
message	*Nachricht, Botschaft*
messenger	*Bote, Botin*
metal	*Metall*
microphone	*Mikrofon*
microwave	*Mikrowelle*
midday	*Mittag*
middle	*Mitte*
midnight	*Mitternacht*
might	*könnte*
mile	*Meile*
milk	*Milch*
mind	*Sinn, Verstand*
(to) mind	*ausmachen (in Sätzen wie: Es macht mir nichts aus …)*
mine	*meine(r, s)*
mine	*Bergwerk*
miner	*Bergarbeiter/-in*
mineral water	*Mineralwasser*
minimum wage	*Mindestlohn*
minority	*Minderheit*
minute	*Minute*
miserable	*elend, unglücklich, erbärmlich*
(to) miss	*vermissen, verpassen*
mission	*Einsatz, Mission*
mist	*Dunst, Nebel*
mistake	*Fehler*
(to) mix	*mischen*
mixture	*Mischung*
(to) moan	*stöhnen, jammern*
mobile home	*Wohnmobil*
mobile phone	*Handy, Mobiltelefon*
model	*Modell*
moderate	*gemäßigt, mäßig*
moment	*Augenblick*
Monday	*Montag*
money	*Geld*
monitor	*Bildschirm*
monkey	*Affe*
monster	*Ungeheuer*
month	*Monat*
mood	*Laune*
moon	*Mond*
moose	*Elch*
more	*mehr, weitere*

morning	*Morgen*
most	*die meisten*
mother	*Mutter*
motion	*Bewegung*
motorbike	*Motorrad*
motorcyclist	*Motorradfahrer/-in*
motorway	*Autobahn*
mountain	*Berg*
mountain biking	*Mountainbiken*
mouse	*Maus*
mouth	*Mund*
(to) move	*sich bewegen, umziehen*
movement	*Bewegung*
movie	*Film*
much	*viel*
mud	*Schlamm*
mug	*Becher*
mum	*Mutti, Mama*
murder	*Mord*
(to) murder	*ermorden*
murderer	*Mörder/-in*
muscle	*Muskel*
music	*Musik*
musician	*Musiker/-in*
mustn't	*darf nicht*
my	*mein(e, s)*
mysterious	*geheimnisvoll*
mystery	*Geheimnis, Rätsel*
name	*Name*
(to) name	*nennen, benennen*
narrow	*eng*
native	*einheimisch, (Ur)Einwohner/-in*
naturally	*natürlich*
nature	*Natur*
near	*nahe, in der Nähe*
nearly	*fast, beinahe*
neat	*ordentlich, sauber*
necessary	*nötig, notwendig*
neck	*Hals*
need	*Bedürfnis, Bedarf*
(to) need	*brauchen*
needn't	*nicht brauchen, nicht müssen*
negative	*negativ, ablehnend*
neighbour	*Nachbar/-in*
neighbourhood	*Nachbarschaft*
neither	*keine(r, s)*
nephew	*Neffe*
nerve	*Nerv*
nervous	*nervös*
net	*Netz, Internet*
never	*nie*
new	*neu*
news	*Nachrichten*
newspaper	*Tageszeitung*
next	*nächste(r, s)*

next to	*neben*
nice	*schön, angenehm*
nickname	*Spitzname*
niece	*Nichte*
night	*Nacht*
nightmare	*Alptraum*
nighttime	*Nacht*
nil	*Null*
noble	*edel, großzügig*
nobody	*niemand*
noise	*Lärm, Krach*
noisy	*laut, lärmend*
(to) nominate	*nominieren, aufstellen*
none	*keine(r, s)*
nonsense	*Unsinn*
non-smoking	*Nichtraucher-*
nor	*auch nicht*
nor do I	*ich auch nicht*
nose	*Nase*
not yet	*noch nicht*
note	*Notiz*
(to) note	*beachten*
note	*Notiz*
notebook	*Notizbuch, tragbarer Computer*
nothing	*nichts*
(to) notice	*jdn./etwas bemerken*
notice board	*Anschlagtafel, schwarzes Brett*
nought	*null*
now	*jetzt*
nowadays	*heutzutage*
nowhere	*nirgends, nirgendwo*
number	*Zahl*
nurse	*Krankenschwester, Krankenpfleger/-in*
nut	*Nuss*
object	*Objekt, Gegenstand, Ziel*
(to) object	*Einspruch erheben*
(to) observe	*beobachten*
(to) obtain	*erhalten*
obvious	*deutlich, offensichtlich*
occasion	*Anlass*
(to) occur	*geschehen*
October	*Oktober*
of course	*natürlich, selbstverständlich*
offence	*Vergehen*
(to) offend	*beleidigen*
offer	*Angebot*
(to) offer	*anbieten*
office	*Büro*
office hours	*Bürozeiten*
officer	*Offizier/-in, Beamte/-r*
official	*offiziell, amtlich*
often	*oft, häufig*

oil	*Öl*
old	*alt*
older	*älter*
old-fashioned	*altmodisch*
Olympic Games	*Olympische Spiele*
once	*einmal*
one	*ein(e, s)*
onion	*Zwiebel*
only	*nur*
on time	*pünktlich*
on TV	*im Fernsehen*
open	*offen*
opening hours	*Öffnungszeiten*
(to) operate	*verkehren, bedienen, operieren*
opinion	*Meinung*
opponent	*Gegner/-in*
opportunity	*(günstige) Gelegenheit*
(to) oppose	*sich wenden gegen, gegen etwas sein*
opposite	*gegenüber, entgegengesetzt, das Gegenteil*
opposition	*Widerstand*
oral	*mündlich*
orchestra	*Orchester*
order	*Befehl*
ordinary	*gewöhnlich*
organization	*Organisation*
(to) organize	*einrichten, ordnen, gliedern*
origin	*Ursprung*
original	*original*
otherwise	*sonst*
ought to	*sollte (eigentlich)*
ours	*unsere(r, s)*
outdoors	*draußen, im Freien*
outfit	*Kleider, Kleidung*
outside	*außen, außerhalb*
over	*über*
(to) overcome	*überwinden*
overcrowded	*überfüllt*
overseas	*Auslands-, ausländisch*
(to) overtake	*überholen*
(to) overwhelm	*überwältigen*
own	*eigen(e)*
(to) own	*besitzen*
owner	*Besitzer/-in*
(to) pack	*(zusammen)packen*
packet	*Paket*
page	*Seite*
pain	*Schmerz*
painful	*schmerzhaft*
(to) paint	*malen*
pair	*Paar*
palace	*Palast*
pale	*bleich, blass*
paper	*Papier, Zeitung*

parade	*Parade, Umzug*
paragraph	*Absatz*
paramedic	*Sanitäter/-in*
pardon	*wie bitte?*
parents	*Eltern*
(to) park	*(Auto) parken*
parliament	*Parlament*
part	*Teil*
part-time	*Teilzeit*
party	*Partei, Feier*
(to) pass	*(eine Prüfung) bestehen; vorbeigehen/-fahren (an)*
passage	*Gang*
passenger	*Passagier, Fahrgast*
passport	*Reisepass, Pass*
password	*Passwort*
past	*vorüber, vorbei*
pastime	*Zeitvertreib*
path	*Weg*
patience	*Geduld*
patient	*geduldig*
pattern	*Muster*
pause	*Pause*
pavement	*Gehweg, Fußweg*
pay	*Bezahlung*
(to) pay (for)	*bezahlen*
payment	*Zahlung, Bezahlung*
pay rise	*Gehaltserhöhung*
PE (Physical Education)	*(Schul)Sport, Sportunterricht*
pea	*Erbse*
peace	*Friede*
peaceful	*friedlich*
peak time	*Hauptverkehrszeit*
peanut	*Erdnuss*
pen	*Stift*
pencil	*Bleistift*
pencilcase	*Federmäppchen*
pen-friend	*Brieffreund/-in*
people	*Menschen, Leute*
per cent	*Prozent*
perfect	*vollkommen*
(to) perform	*aufführen, vorführen*
performance	*(Film-, Theater-)Vorstellung, Leistung*
perhaps	*vielleicht*
period	*Zeitspanne*
persecution	*Verfolgung*
permission	*Erlaubnis*
personnel	*Personal, Belegschaft*
(to) persuade	*überzeugen, überreden*
pet	*Haustier*
petrol [BE]	*Benzin*
petrol station [BE]	*Tankstelle*
phone	*Telefon*
(to) phone	*anrufen*

(to) phone friends	*Freunde anrufen*
(to) be on the phone	*telefonieren*
(to) photocopy	*fotokopieren*
phrase	*Wendung, Ausdruck*
physical	*körperlich*
Physical Education (PE)	*(Schul)Sport, Sportunterricht*
physical science	*Naturwissenschaft*
physics	*Physik*
piano	*Klavier*
(to) pick	*(Früchte) pflücken, etwas abholen, aufheben*
picnic	*Picknick*
picture	*Bild*
piece	*Stück*
pig	*Schwein*
pill	*Tablette*
pilot	*Pilot/-in*
pin	*Stecknadel, Anstecker*
pink	*rosa*
pipe	*Pfeife*
pity	*Mitleid*
(to) pity	*bemitleiden*
place	*Platz, Ort, Stelle*
place of birth	*Geburtsort*
plain	*einfach, schlicht*
plan	*Plan*
(to) plan	*planen*
plane	*Flugzeug*
planet	*Planet*
plant	*Pflanze*
(to) plant	*pflanzen*
plate	*Teller*
platform	*Bahnsteig, Gleis*
play	*Spiel, Theaterstück*
(to) play	*spielen*
(to) play a musical instrument	*ein Musikinstrument spielen*
(to) play in a band	*in einer Band spielen*
(to) play on the computer	*am Computer spielen*
(to) play the guitar	*Gitarre spielen*
(to) play the piano	*Klavier spielen*
playing field	*Spielplatz*
pleasant	*angenehm*
(to) please	*jdm. gefallen*
pleased	*zufrieden*
pleasure	*Vergnügen*
plenty	*zahlreich, mehr als genug*
plug	*Stecker*
p.m.	*nachmittags, abends*
pocket	*Tasche*
poem	*Gedicht*

(to) point	*zeigen, deuten (auf)*
poison	*Gift*
police	*Polizei*
polite	*höflich*
political	*politisch*
politician	*Politiker/-in*
politics	*Politik*
(to) pollute	*verschmutzen*
pollution	*(Umwelt)Verschmutzung*
poor	*arm*
popular	*beliebt*
population	*Bevölkerung*
pork	*Schweinefleisch*
port	*Hafen(stadt)*
position	*Stellung, Lage*
positive	*sicher, bestimmt*
(to) possess	*besitzen*
possession	*Besitz*
possibility	*Möglichkeit*
possible	*möglich*
(to) post	*auf die Post geben*
postman	*Briefträger, Postbote*
pot	*Kanne, Topf*
potato	*Kartoffel*
(to) pour	*gießen*
power	*Kraft, Stärke*
powerful	*mächtig*
practical	*praktisch*

practice	*Übung*
(to) practise [BE], **(to) practice** [AE]	*üben*
(to) practise (a sport / hobby)	*ausüben*
(to) pray	*beten*
prayer	*Gebet*
precise	*genau, präzise*
(to) prefer	*(etwas) vorziehen*
preparation	*Vorbereitung*
(to) prepare	*(sich) vorbereiten*
(to) present	*überreichen, schenken*
present	*Geschenk*
present	*gegenwärtig, momentan*
presenter	*Moderator/-in*
president	*Präsident/-in*
(to) press	*bügeln*
pressure	*(nervlicher) Druck*
pretty	*hübsch, ziemlich*
(to) prevent	*verhindern*
previous	*vorhergehend*
price	*Preis*
pride	*Stolz*
primary school	*Grundschule*
prime minister	*Premierminister/-in*
prince	*Prinz*
princess	*Prinzessin*
(to) print	*drucken*

printer	*Drucker*
printout	*Ausdruck*
prison	*Gefängnis*
prize	*Preis (= Gewinn), Auszeichnung*
probable	*wahrscheinlich*
process	*Ablauf*
(to) process	*verarbeiten, bearbeiten*
(to) produce	*herstellen*
production	*Herstellung*
professional	*Profi-, Berufs-(Sportler/-in)*
profit	*Gewinn*
progress	*Fortschritt*
project	*Projekt, Vorhaben*
promise	*Versprechen*
(to) promise	*versprechen*
(to) pronounce	*aussprechen*
proof	*Beweis*
proper	*passend, richtig, geeignet*
properly	*anständig, angemessen*
(to) propose	*vorschlagen*
(to) protect	*(be)schützen*
protection	*Schutz*
protest	*Protest*
(to) protest	*protestieren*
proud	*stolz*
(to) prove	*beweisen*
(to) provide	*sorgen (für), versorgen*
public	*öffentlich*
public transport	*öffentliche Verkehrsmittel*
(to) pull down	*(ein Haus) abreißen*
(to) punish	*bestrafen*
pupil	*Schüler/-in*
pure	*rein, pur*
(to) push	*schieben, stoßen*
(to) put	*legen, stellen, legen*
quality	*Qualität, Güte*
quantity	*Menge*
quarter	*Viertel*
queen	*Königin*
question	*Frage*
(to) question	*infrage stellen*
questionnaire	*Fragebogen*
quick	*schnell*
quiet	*still, ruhig*
quite	*ganz, ziemlich*
quote	*Zitat*
(to) quote	*zitieren*
rabbit	*Kaninchen*
race	*Rennen*
racing	*(Pferde)Rennen*
radio	*Radio*
on the radio	*im Radio*

rail	*Bahn, Gleis, Schiene*
by rail	*mit der Bahn*
railway	*Eisenbahn*
rain	*Regen*
(to) raise	*aufziehen, großziehen*
range	*Auswahl*
rank	*Rang*
rare	*selten*
rarely	*selten, nicht oft*
rat	*Ratte*
rather	*lieber, ziemlich*
(to) rattle	*rütteln*
raw	*roh, unbehandelt*
RE (Religious Education)	*Religion(sunterricht)*
(to) reach	*erreichen*
(to) react	*reagieren*
reaction	*Reaktion*
(to) read	*lesen*
ready	*fertig, bereit*
real	*wirklich, real*
(to) realise	*erkennen, feststellen*
reality	*Realität, Wirklichkeit*
really	*unbedingt*
reason	*Grund, Anlass*
reasonable	*vernünftig, angemessen*
(to) rebuild	*wieder aufbauen*
(to) receive	*erhalten, bekommen*
recent	*jüngst, neulich*
recently	*neulich, in letzter Zeit*
receptionist	*Empfangschef, Empfangsdame (im Hotel)*
(to) recognise	*erkennen*
(to) recommend	*empfehlen*
(to) record	*aufzeichnen, aufnehmen*
(to) recover	*sich erholen, gesund werden*
(to) recycle	*wiederverwerten, aufbereiten*
red	*rot*
(to) reduce	*herabsetzen, verringern*
(to) refer (to)	*sich beziehen (auf)*
(to) refuse	*abschlagen, sich weigern*
(to) regard	*betrachten*
region	*Region, Bezirk, Bereich*
regret	*Bedauern*
(to) regret	*bedauern*
regular	*regelmäßig*
rehearsal	*Probe*
(to) reject	*etwas ablehnen*
(to) be related	*verwandt sein*
relationship	*Beziehung*
relative	*Verwandte/-r*

(to) relax	*sich ausruhen, entspannen*
reliable	*zuverlässig*
remark	*Bemerkung*
(to) remark	*äußern, bemerken*
(to) remember	*sich erinnern, denken an*
(to) remind (of)	*jdn. erinnern (an)*
(to) remove	*beseitigen, entfernen*
rent	*Miete*
(to) rent	*mieten, leihen*
(to) repair	*reparieren*
(to) repeat	*wiederholen*
(to) replace	*ersetzen*
reply	*Antwort*
(to) reply	*antworten*
report	*Bericht*
(to) report (on)	*berichten (über)*
reporter	*Reporter/-in*
(to) represent	*vertreten*
reputation	*Ruf, Ansehen*
(to) rescue	*retten*
research	*Forschung*
reservation	*Reservierung*
(to) reserve	*reservieren, zurückhalten, aufheben*
respect	*Hinsicht*
responsibility	*Verantwortung*
responsible	*verantwortlich*
rest	*Ruhe(pause)*
result	*Ergebnis*
(to) return	*zurückkommen*
review	*(Buch-, Film-)Besprechung*
revision exercise	*Wiederholungsübung*
rhyme	*Reim*
rice	*Reis*
rich	*reich*
ride	*Spazierfahrt*
(to) ride	*reiten, fahren*
(to) ride a bike	*mit dem Fahrrad fahren*
riding	*Reiten*
right	*richtig, direkt, gerade, rechts*
(to) ring	*klingeln, läuten, anrufen*
(to) ring the bell	*klingeln*
(to) rise	*(an-, auf-)steigen, aufgehen (Sonne)*
risk	*Risiko*
(to) risk	*riskieren*
rival	*Rivale, Rivalin, Konkurrent/-in*
river	*Fluss*
road	*(Land)Straße*
road works	*Straßenbauarbeiten*
(to) rob	*be-, ausrauben*
robot	*Roboter*
rocket	*Rakete*
role	*Rolle*

(to) roll	*rollen*
romantic	*romantisch*
roof	*Dach*
room	*Zimmer, Raum*
rope	*Seil, Tau*
rough	*rau, grob*
round	*rund; um … herum, Runde*
route	*Route, Strecke*
(to) rub	*reiben*
rubber [BE]	*Radiergummi*
rubbish	*Müll*
rude	*unhöflich*
(to) ruin	*ruinieren, zerstören*
rule	*Vorschrift, Regel*
ruler	*Lineal*
rumour	*Gerücht*
(to) run	*rennen, laufen*
(to) run in the family	*in der Familie liegen*
(to) run out of sth.	*ausgehen, etwas nicht mehr haben*
runner	*Läufer/-in*
(to) rush	*eilen, hetzen*
rush hour	*Hauptverkehrszeit*
sad	*traurig, betrübt*
safe	*sicher*
safety	*Sicherheit*
(to) sail	*segeln*
salad	*Salat*
salary	*Gehalt*
sale	*Verkauf*
for sale	*zu verkaufen*
sales	*Schlussverkauf, Verkauf, Vertrieb*
same	*der-, die-, dasselbe*
sandwich	*belegtes Brot*
(to) satisfy	*zufriedenstellen*
Saturday	*Samstag*
saucer	*Untertasse*
sausage	*Wurst, Würstchen*
(to) save	*speichern, retten, sparen*
(to) say	*sagen*
scared	*verängstigt, erschrocken*
scarf, scarves [Pl.]	*Schal, Halstuch*
scary	*gruselig, unheimlich*
scene	*Szene*
schedule	*Programm*
scholarship	*Stipendium*
school	*Schule*
school fees	*Schulgeld, Schulgebühren*
school holiday(s)	*Schulferien*
school leaver	*Schulabgänger/-in*
school meal	*(Mittag)Essen in der Schule*
school report	*Zeugnis*

school trip	*Schulfahrt, Klassenreise*
school uniform	*Schuluniform*
science	*Naturwissenschaft*
scientist	*(Natur)Wissenschaftler/-in*
scissors	*Schere*
score	*Punktestand, Spielstand*
scrapbook	*Sammelalbum*
scream	*Schrei*
(to) scream	*schreien*
screen	*Bildschirm*
script	*Drehbuch*
sea	*Meer, die See*
seal	*Robbe, Seehund*
(to) search	*suchen*
search engine	*Suchmaschine*
seasick	*seekrank*
at the seaside	*am Meer*
season	*Jahreszeit*
seat	*(Sitz)Platz*
seatbelt	*Gurt*
second	*Sekunde, zweite(r, s)*
secret	*Geheimnis*
secretary	*Sekrektär/-in*
section	*Abschnitt, Teil*
(to) see	*sehen*
seed	*Saat, Same*
(to) seem	*scheinen*
(to) sell	*verkaufen*
(to) send	*senden*
sense	*Sinn, Verstand*
sense of humor	*Sinn für Humor*
sensible	*vernünftig*
sensitive	*sensibel, empfindlich*
sentence	*Satz*
(to) separate	*trennen, (ab)teilen*
separate	*getrennt, abgesondert*
separated	*getrennt*
serious	*ernst(haft)*
(to) serve	*dienen, servieren*
(to) serve	*servieren*
service	*Bedienung, Dienst*
(to) set an example	*ein Beispiel geben*
(to) set up	*aufschlagen*
(to) settle	*sich niederlassen, besiedeln*
settlement	*Siedlung, Niederlassung*
several	*mehrere, verschiedene*
shade	*Schatten*
shadow	*Schatten*
(to) shake	*schütteln, zittern*
shame	*Schande, Schamgefühl*
shape	*Form, Gestalt*
(to) share	*teilen*
sharp	*scharf*

shawl	Schultertuch
sheep	Schaf
shelf, shelves [Pl.]	Regal
shelter	Schutz
(to) shine	glänzen, scheinen
ship	Schiff
shirt	Hemd
shock	Schock
(to) shock	einen Schock versetzen, schockieren
shoe	Schuh
(to) shoot	schießen, erschießen
shop	Laden
shop assistant	Verkäufer/-in
shoplifter	Ladendieb/-in
shopping	Einkaufen
(to) do the shopping	einkaufen gehen
shore	Küste, Ufer
short	kurz
shorts	kurze Hosen, Shorts
shot	Schuss
should	sollte
shoulder	Schulter
(to) shout	rufen, (an)schreien
(to) show	zeigen
shower	Dusche
(to) shut	schließen
shy	schüchtern, scheu
sick	krank
side	Seite
sidewalk [AE]	Gehweg
sight	Sehenswürdigkeit
sign	Zeichen
(to) sign	unterschreiben
signal	Signal, Zeichen
(to) signal	blinken
signature	Unterschrift
silence	Ruhe, Stille
silly	dumm
simple	einfach
since	seit
(to) sing	singen
single	ledig
(to) sink	sinken, untergehen
sister	Schwester
(to) sit	sitzen
site	Seite
situation	Lage, Situation
size	Größe
(to) skateboard	Skateboard fahren
skateboarding	Skateboardfahren
(to) ski	Ski fahren
skiing	Skifahren
skilful	geschickt, gewandt
skill	Fähigkeit, Fertigkeit
skin	Haut
skinny	mager, dürr

skirt	*Rock*
sky	*Himmel*
skyline	*Silhouette, Skyline*
slave	*Sklave, Sklavin*
sledge	*Schlitten*
sleep	*Schlaf*
(to) sleep	*schlafen*
sleeping bag	*Schlafsack*
(to) slide	*gleiten, rutschen*
slight	*schwach, klein, unbedeutend*
slim	*schlank*
(to) slip	*ausrutschen und hinfallen*
slogan	*Werbespruch*
slope	*Hang*
slow	*langsam*
small	*klein*
smart	*schlau, clever, intelligent*
smell	*Geruch*
(to) smell	*riechen*
smile	*Lächeln*
(to) smile	*lächeln*
smoke	*Rauch*
(to) smoke	*rauchen*
smooth	*glatt*
SMS (short message system)	*SMS, Kurznachricht*
snake	*Schlange*
snow	*Schnee*
(to) snow	*schneien*
(to) soak	*einweichen*
soap	*Seife*
sober	*nüchtern*
soccer	*(europäischer) Fußball*
society	*Gesellschaft*
sock	*Socke, Strumpf*
so far	*bisher*
soft	*weich*
soft drink	*alkoholfreies Getränk*
software programme	*Computerprogramm*
soil	*Erdboden*
solar	*Sonnen-*
solar energy	*Sonnenenergie*
soldier	*Soldat/-in*
(to) solve	*lösen, auflösen*
some	*einige, irgendein*
somebody	*jemand*
somehow	*irgendwie*
sometimes	*manchmal*
son	*Sohn*
song	*Lied*
soon	*bald*
sore	*wund*
sorry	*es tut mir leid*

sort	*Sorte*
sound	*Ton, Geräusch*
soup	*Suppe*
source	*Quelle*
space	*Raum, Platz*
(to) spare	*jdn. verschonen*
spark	*Funke*
(to) speak	*sprechen, reden*
(to) speak up	*lauter sprechen*
speaker	*Sprecher/-in*
special	*besondere*
spectator	*Zuschauer/-in*
speech	*Rede*
(to) make a speech	*eine Rede halten*
speed	*Geschwindigkeit*
speed limit	*Geschwindigkeitsbegrenzung*
(to) spell	*buchstabieren, richtig schreiben*
spelling	*Rechtschreibung*
spelling mistake	*Rechtschreibfehler*
(to) spend	*(Zeit) verbringen*
(to) spend money (on)	*(Geld) ausgeben (für)*
spicy	*würzig, stark gewürzt*
(to) spill	*verschütten*
(to) spin	*schleudern, drehen*
spirit	*Geist*
(to) split	*teilen, spalten*
(to) spoil	*verderben, verschandeln*
spoon	*Löffel*
sport	*Sport, Sportart*
sportsman	*Sportler, Athlet*
sportswoman	*Sportlerin, Athletin*
spot	*Fleck*
(to) spot	*entdecken*
(to) spread	*ausbreiten, verteilen*
spring	*Frühling*
(to) spring	*springen*
square	*öffentlicher Platz, Viereck*
(to) squash	*zerdrücken*
stadium	*Stadion*
staff	*Personal*
staff room	*Lehrerzimmer*
stage	*Bühne*
stain	*Fleck*
staircase	*Treppenhaus*
stairs	*Treppe*
stall	*Stand*
stamp	*Briefmarke*
(to) stand	*stehen*
star	*Stern, Star*
(to) start	*anfangen, beginnen*
start	*Anfang, Beginn*
(to) start a family	*eine Familie gründen*
(to) start on sth.	*mit etwas anfangen*

state	*Staat*
statement	*Aussage, Behauptung*
station	*Bahnhof*
statue	*Statue*
status	*Status, Rang*
stay	*Aufenthalt*
(to) stay	*beiben*
(to) stay at a hotel	*in einem Hotel übernachten / wohnen*
steady	*stetig, fest, standhaft*
(to) steal	*stehlen*
steam	*Dampf*
step	*Schritt, Stufe*
stepmother	*Stiefmutter*
stick	*Zweig*
(to) stick	*kleben*
stiff	*steif*
still	*noch*
sting	*Stachel, Stich*
(to) sting	*stechen*
(to) stir	*(sich) rühren, sich regen*
stomach	*Magen*
stone	*Stein*
(to) stop	*aufhören*
store	*Laden, Geschäft*
(to) store	*speichern*
store room	*Lagerraum*
storey [BE], **story** [AE]	*Etage*
storm	*Sturm*
story	*Geschichte*
straight	*gerade*
strange	*fremdartig, seltsam*
stream	*Bach*
street	*Straße*
strength	*Kraft, Stärke*
stress	*Stress*
(to) stress	*belasten*
(to) stretch	*sich erstrecken*
strict	*streng*
strike	*Streik*
string	*Schnur, Bindfaden*
strong	*stark*
(to) be / get stuck	*stecken bleiben*
student	*Student/-in, Schüler/-in*
study	*Studie*
(to) study	*erforschen, lernen, studieren*
(to) study a map	*eine Karte studieren*
stuff	*Zeug, Kram*
stupid	*dumm, blöd*
subject	*Thema, Gegenstand, Schulfach*
suburb	*Vorort*
subway	*U-Bahn [AE], Unterführung [BE]*
(to) succeed	*Erfolg haben*

success	*Erfolg*
successful	*erfolgreich*
such	*solche*
suddenly	*plötzlich, auf einmal*
(to) suffer from	*leiden an*
sugar	*Zucker*
(to) suggest	*vorschlagen*
suggestion	*Vorschlag*
suit	*Anzug*
(to) suit	*passen*
sum	*Summe*
summer	*Sommer*
sun	*Sonne*
sunny	*sonnig*
supermarket	*Supermarkt*
supper	*Abendessen*
supply	*Angebot, Vorrat*
(to) supply	*liefern*
(to) support	*unterstützen*
supporter	*Fan, Anhänger/-in*
(to) suppose	*annehmen, vermuten*
sure	*natürlich, sicherlich*
surface	*Oberfläche*
(to) surf	*surfen*
(to) surf the internet	*im Internet surfen*
surprise	*Überraschung*
(to) surprise	*überraschen*
survey	*Umfrage, Studie*
(to) survive	*überleben*
suspect	*Verdächtige/-r*
(to) suspect	*verdächtigen, ahnen*
(to) swallow	*schlucken*
sweat	*Schweiß*
(to) sweat	*schwitzen*
(to) sweep	*fegen, kehren*
sweet	*süß*
(to) swim	*schwimmen*
swing	*Schaukel*
(to) swing	*schwingen*
switch	*Schalter*
(to) switch	*(um)schalten*
(to) switch off	*ausschalten*
(to) switch on	*einschalten*
table	*Tisch*
(to) take	*nehmen*
(to) take a break	*eine Pause machen*
(to) take an exam	*eine Prüfung machen*
(to) take notes	*Notizen machen, mitschreiben*
(to) take part in	*teilnehmen an*
(to) take s.o. to school	*jdn. in die Schule bringen*
(to) take sth. to the post	*etwas zur Post bringen*
(to) take the rubbish out	*den Müll hinausbringen*
(to) take time	*Zeit kosten, dauern*

tale	*Erzählung*
talent	*Begabung*
talk	*Gespräch*
(to) talk	*sprechen*
tall	*groß*
target	*Ziel(scheibe)*
task	*Aufgabe*
taste	*Geschmack*
(to) taste	*schmecken*
tax	*Steuer*
tea	*Tee*
(to) teach	*unterrichten, lehren*
team	*Mannschaft*
(to) be on a team	*in einer Mannschaft sein*
(to) tear	*(zer)reißen*
technical	*technisch, technologisch*
technology	*Technik, Technologie*
teenager	*Jugendliche/-r*
teeth [Pl. von tooth]	*Zähne*
telephone	*Telefon*
television	*Fernsehgerät*
(to) tell	*erzählen*
temperature	*Temperatur*
tense	*Zeitform*
tent	*Zelt*
term	*Bedingung, Trimester*
terrible	*schrecklich*
test	*Prüfung*
(to) test	*prüfen, testen*
(to) text	*eine SMS/Kurznachricht senden*
textbook	*Lehrbuch*
text message	*SMS, Kurznachricht*
than	*als (nach Komparativ)*
(to) thank	*danken*
Thanksgiving	*amerikanisches Erntedankfest*
theatre	*Theater*
their	*ihr(e)*
theme park	*Freizeitpark, Vergnügungspark*
then	*dann, damals*
theory	*Theorie*
there	*da, dort*
there is/are	*es gibt*
these	*diese*
thief, thieves [Pl.]	*Dieb/-in*
thin	*dünn*
thing	*Ding*
(to) think	*denken*
third	*dritte(r, s)*
thirst	*Durst*
thirsty	*durstig*
thorough	*gründlich*
those	*die da, jene dort*
though	*obwohl*

thought	Gedanke
thousand	tausend
threat	Bedrohung
(to) threaten	bedrohen
thriller	Krimi
throat	Kehle
through	durch
(to) throw	werfen
thumb	Daumen
Thursday	Donnerstag
(to) tick	ankreuzen
ticket	Eintrittskarte, Fahrkarte, Ticket
tidy	ordentlich
(to) tidy up	aufräumen
tie	Krawatte
(to) tie	binden
tight	eng, dicht
till (until)	bis
time	Zeit
(to) be on time	pünktlich sein
(to) have a good time	sich amüsieren
(to) have a great time	Spaß haben
(to) take time	dauern, Zeit kosten
What time is it?	Wie spät ist es?
timetable	Stundenplan, Fahrplan
tin [BE]	Dose, Büchse
tip	Trinkgeld, Rat, Tipp
tired	müde
title	Überschrift, Titel
today	heute
toe	Zehe
together	zusammen
toilet	Toilette
tomorrow	morgen
tongue	Zunge
tonight	heute Abend
tool(s)	Werkzeug
toolbox	Werkzeugkasten
tooth, teeth [Pl.]	Zahn
toothache	Zahnschmerzen
toothbrush	Zahnbürste
top	oberes Ende, Spitze, Top (Shirt)
topic	Thema
total	Gesamtbetrag, Summe
totally	völlig
touch	Berührung
(to) touch	berühren
tough	zäh
tour (of)	(Rund)Reise (durch)
tourism	Tourismus
tourist	Tourist/-in
tourist attraction	Touristenattraktion
towards	in Richtung auf

tower	*Turm*
town	*Stadt*
toy	*Spielzeug*
track	*(Fuß)Spur*
track and field	*Leichtathletik*
tracksuit	*Jogginganzug*
trade	*Handel, Beruf*
(to) trade	*handeln*
trade fair	*Messe*
tradition	*Überlieferung, Tradition*
traffic	*Verkehr*
traffic jam	*Verkehrsstau*
traffic lights	*Verkehrsampel*
train	*Zug*
(to) train	*trainieren, eine Ausbildung machen*
trainee	*Auszubildende/-r*
trainer	*Trainer/-in, Ausbilder/-in*
trainers	*Turnschuhe*
training	*Ausbildung*
tram	*Straßenbahn*
(to) translate	*übersetzen*
translation	*Übersetzung*
transparency	*Folie*
transport	*Verkehr, Verkehrsmittel*
trap	*Falle*
travel	*Reise*
(to) travel	*reisen*
travel agency	*Reisebüro*
(to) tread	*treten*
(to) treat	*behandeln*
treatment	*Behandlung*
tree	*Baum*
trend	*Richtung*
trick	*Streich*
(to) trick	*jdm. einen Streich spielen*
trip (to)	*Reise (nach)*
trouble	*Problem, Schwierigkeit*
trousers	*Hose*
true	*wahr*
(to) trust	*vertrauen*
truth	*Wahrheit*
try	*Versuch*
(to) try	*versuchen*
tube	*Londons U-Bahn*
Tuesday	*Dienstag*
tune	*Lied, Melodie*
turn	*Drehung, Kurve*
(to) turn	*drehen*
(to) turn off	*ausschalten, abschalten*
(to) turn on	*einschalten*
TV	*Fernsehen, Fernseher*
TV set	*Fernsehgerät*
on TV	*im Fernsehen*

twice	*zweimal*
twin	*Zwilling*
(to) type in	*eintippen*
typical (of)	*typisch (für)*
umbrella	*Regenschirm*
unable	*unfähig, nicht in der Lage*
uncertain	*unsicher*
uncle	*Onkel*
uncomfortable	*unbequem*
under	*unter*
underground	*Untergrund, U-Bahn*
(to) underline	*unterstreichen*
underneath	*unter*
(to) understand	*verstehen*
(to) undo	*öffnen, etwas rückgängig machen*
unemployed	*arbeitslos*
unemployment	*Arbeitslosigkeit*
unfair	*ungerecht*
unfortunate	*unglücklich*
unfriendly	*unfreundlich*
unhappy	*unglücklich*
unhealthy	*ungesund*
uniform	*Uniform*
unimportant	*unwichtig*
unit	*Lektion, Einheit*
(to) unite	*(sich) vereinigen*
university	*Universität*
unkind	*unfreundlich*
unknown	*unbekannt, nicht bekannt*
unless	*wenn nicht*
(to) unpack	*auspacken*
unpleasant	*unerfreulich*
unpopular	*unbeliebt*
unsafe	*unsicher*
unskilled	*ungelernt*
unskilled worker	*Hilfsarbeiter/-in*
untidy	*unordentlich*
until	*bis*
unusual	*ungewöhnlich*
unwanted	*unerwünscht, störend*
upset	*aufgebracht, aufgeregt*
(to) upset	*aufregen, aufwiegeln*
upside-down	*verkehrt herum, auf dem Kopf*
upstairs	*oben, nach oben*
urgent	*dringend*
(to) use	*gebrauchen, nutzen*
(to) be used to	*gewöhnt sein (an)*
useful	*nützlich*
useless	*nutzlos*
usual	*gewöhnlich*
vacation [AE]	*Ferien, Urlaub*
valley	*Tal*
value	*Wert*
(to) value	*wertschätzen*

van	*Transporter, Lieferwagen*
vandalism	*Zerstörungswut*
(to) vanish	*verschwinden*
variety	*Auswahl, Mannigfaltigkeit*
various	*verschieden*
vegetable	*Gemüse*
vegetarian	*Vegetarier/-in*
vehicle	*Fahrzeug*
very	*sehr*
victim	*Opfer*
victory	*Sieg*
view	*Ansicht, Meinung, Aussicht*
viewer	*Zuschauer/-in*
village	*Dorf*
violence	*Gewalt, Gewalttätigkeit*
violent	*gewalttätig, heftig*
virtual	*so gut wie, nicht wirklich vorhanden, virtuell*
vision	*Sehvermögen, Vorstellung, Einbildung*
visit	*Besuch*
(to) visit	*besuchen*
visitor	*Besucher/-in*
vocabulary	*Wortschatz, Vokabular*
voice	*Stimme*
volleyball	*Volleyball*
volunteer	*Freiwillige/-r*
vote	*Stimmrecht, Stimme*
(to) vote	*abstimmen; wählen*
voyage	*Schiffsreise*
wage	*Lohn*
(to) wait	*warten*
waiter	*Kellner, Bedienung*
waitress	*Kellnerin, Bedienung*
(to) wake up	*aufwachen*
walk	*Spaziergang*
(to) walk	*laufen, gehen, spazieren gehen*
wall	*Mauer, Wand*
wallet	*Brieftasche*
wallpaper	*Tapete*
(to) want	*(haben) wollen*
war	*Krieg*
wardrobe	*Kleiderschrank*
warm	*warm*
(to) warn	*warnen*
(to) wash	*waschen*
washbasin	*Waschbecken*
(to) wash the dishes	*Geschirr spülen*
waste	*Abfall*
(to) waste	*verschwenden*
waste of time	*Zeitverschwendung*
waste water	*Abwasser*

(to) watch	*sehen*
(to) watch birds	*Vögel beobachten*
(to) watch out	*aufpassen*
Watch out!	*Achtung!*
(to) watch sport on TV	*Sport im Fernsehen sehen*
(to) watch TV	*fernsehen*
water	*Wasser*
water sport	*Wassersport*
wave	*Welle*
wax	*Wachs*
way	*Weg*
weak	*schwach*
wealth	*Wohlstand*
wealthy	*wohlhabend, reich*
weapon	*Waffe*
(to) wear	*(Kleid, Uniform) tragen*
weather	*Wetter*
weather forecast	*Wettervorhersage, Wetterbericht*
website	*Seite im Internet*
wedding	*Hochzeit*
wedding anniversary	*Hochzeitstag*
Wednesday	*Mittwoch*
week	*Woche*
weekday	*Wochentag, Werktag*
weekend	*Wochenende*
(to) weigh	*wiegen*
weight	*Gewicht*
welcome	*willkommen*
Welsh	*walisisch, aus Wales*
wet	*nass*
wet paint	*frisch gestrichen*
whale	*Wal*
wheel	*Rad*
wheelchair	*Rollstuhl*
when	*wann*
where	*wo*
whereas	*wohingegen, während*
wherever	*wohin auch immer*
whether	*ob*
while	*während*
whisper	*Geflüster*
(to) whisper	*flüstern*
whistle	*Pfeife, Pfiff*
(to) whistle	*pfeifen*
white	*weiß*
whole	*ganz*
wholly	*gänzlich*
wide	*breit*
widow	*Witwe*
widower	*Witwer*
wife	*Ehefrau*
(to) win	*gewinnen*
window	*Fenster*
wing	*Flügel, Gebäudetrakt*

(to) wipe	*(ab)wischen, (ab)trocknen*
wire	*Draht*
wise	*weise, klug*
wish	*Wunsch*
(to) wish	*wünschen*
within	*drin, im Inneren, innerhalb*
without	*ohne*
witness	*Zeuge, Zeugin*
woman	*Frau*
wonder	*Wunder*
(to) wonder	*sich fragen, sich wundern über*
wonderful	*wunderbar*
wood	*Holz*
word	*Wort*
(to) work	*arbeiten*
(to) work out	*trainieren*
(to) be out of work	*arbeitslos sein*
worksheet	*Arbeitsblatt*
workshop	*Werkstatt*
world	*Welt*
worried	*beunruhigt, besorgt*
(to) worry about	*sich Sorgen machen über*
worse	*schlechter, schlimmer*
worst	*der/die/das schlechteste*
worth	*wert (sein)*
wound	*Wunde*
(to) write	*schreiben*
wrong	*falsch, unrecht*
(to) yawn	*gähnen*
year	*Jahr*
yellow	*gelb*
yesterday	*gestern*
young	*jung*
youngster	*Jugendliche/-r*
Yours sincerely	*Mit freundichen Grüßen*
youth	*Jugend, Jugendliche/-r*
youth club	*Jugendclub*
youth hostel	*Jugendherberge*
(to) zap	*hin- und herschalten*
zero	*Null*
zoo	*Tierpark, Zoo*